A TIME TO RUN FREE

Adventures from my Childhood

JEFFERY CAMPBELL

A Time to Run Free: Adventures from My Childhood

ISBN 978-0-9765890-7-5

Published by the estate of Jeffery Campbell

with the assistance of
Dovetailed Press LLC
5263 North Shore Drive
Duluth, MN 55804

The photographs in this book are from the collection
of the family of Jeffery Campbell.

For additional copies, contact ~

The Estate of Jeffery Campbell
218.722.9990

Cover & interior design ~ Marlene Wisuri

Printed in U. S. A.

In loving memory of my Uncle Tommy who inspired me...

Once in my room he said, "Jeff, we are here for a short time so we should all leave our mark." Uncle Tommy wrote a book and had it published. How I wish he were still around to read mine.

Uncle Tommy

I never married or had children of my own, but somehow through the people who have come and gone throughout my life, I do have an extended family—maybe larger than most. To those of you who have entered my life, this one's for you!

With thanks to Jeff's friend Pam Stolan for all of her long hours and dedication in helping him finish this book.

"I have fought the good fight. I have finished the race. I have kept the faith." *II Timothy 4:7*

INTRODUCTION ❧

My friend Mike and I turned up that all too familiar road, now paved and houses built where grassy fields with wild flowers once grew. Further ahead, was a place full of weeds and small trees that I remembered held a bountiful crop of corn. I could see that old mailbox still standing, rusty, ready for the postman as we turned into the driveway. On the left side, stood the old farmhouse with its windows and doors boarded up. Down below, the garage and barn half torn down. To my right, was the well with its pump handle up as if waiting to give fresh water. Nearby, with its leaves all gone now, stood the apple tree with a long ladder leaning against it, which my old friend used to harvest the fruit. For a moment in time, I forgot all about my wheelchair and paralysis as the memories rushed back.

ONE

It was one of those cold summer nights late in September, the kind that tells you summer is leaving and fall is just beginning. Mom cooked spaghetti that evening so the kitchen and dining room were rich with the smell of Italian seasoning and tomato sauce. All the windows in the surrounding area were steamed up from the pasta boiling on the stove.

My younger brother, Jim, and I were in the basement; Dad's workbench was down there. We decided to take out our .22 rifles and clean them. After taking the rifles out of their cases Mom had made last year for Christmas, we laid them across the old workbench. I jumped up and sat there while Jimmy was sitting on a fold-out steel chair and opened the gun cleaning kit. The room smelled sweet of gun cleaning solvent as we ran the patches through the barrel. We were quiet, probably because we were dreaming about the squirrels and rabbits we were going to shoot when Dad took us hunting. Interrupting us, Mom yelled, "Supper's ready!" We set the .22s down and ran up the stairs into the dining room.

Jimmy and I sat down with my four sisters—Jackie, Annette, Sherry, and Kristie—at the table and with Mom and Dad. On the table there was a big bowl of pasta and another of sauce, a plate of dinner rolls and a bowl of salad. We never talked much during suppertime. Everything was quiet except the usual sounds of silverware making that noise and cups being set down on the table.

The phone rang during our dinner. I heard my dad talking to our neighbor friend Irvin, who I always called Uncle Irvin. Dad seemed to get excited during the conversation. He hurried up and got off the phone, walked back over to the table and said to all of us that Irvin shot a huge bear. Hearing the news, the three of us—Dad, Jimmy, and I—finished our dinners fast and headed out the door. Dad started up the old Ford station wagon. We backed out of the driveway and took off.

Irvin lived only a mile and a half away but it seemed like we just couldn't get there fast enough. It was getting dark by then. Finally, we were on the road that he lived. As we pulled up, the headlights shone on the old mailbox before his driveway. We turned right and pulled up to his house quietly. As we got out of the car we closed the doors gently and walked over to the old farmhouse, knocked on the door, opened it and went in. As we entered there were gunny sacks of potatoes on the right and a pile of squash on the left, a couple of feet after that were newspapers spread out on the cement floor with muddy footprints all over them.

Irvin was sitting in his kitchen with his Remington 870 resting on the table. I remember the old silver flashlight he had duct-taped on the end of the barrel.

Dad said, "So, you shot a bear."

"Yep, it's laying in the backyard under the apple tree."

Irvin then got up from his chair and we all went outside, walked to the backyard and sure enough there was the bear, dead, with one 12-gauge slug right through the shoulders. It looked like every leaf on the apple tree was covered with blood and the exit hole on the bear's shoulder was big enough to put your fist in it.

As the four of us were standing there, Irvin said, "Yeah, I've got bees out back so they can make some honey for me to sell this fall, but this bear has been getting into the hives, tearing them apart and eating the honey. I have a lot of money tied up into the colony so I had to stop it from happening sooner or later."

My dad said, "Well, you gotta do what you gotta do."

"Well Jeff," Irvin said with a grin, "What should we do with it?"

I wasn't really listening at that time, I was remembering the many stories I read in *Field and Stream* and *Outdoor Life* magazines about bear hunting. I always thought it would be exciting to have a bear skin rug and a freezer full of bear steaks that I could cook over a fire, and I imagined I was a mountain man.

Before I could answer Irvin's question, my dad said, "Why don't you skin the bear out and make a rug?" I agreed. So Irvin walked down to the barn and got his 1934 Allis Chalmers tractor, drove it up the driveway into the backyard next to the bear. We put a chain around the bear's back leg and then to the bucket on the front of the tractor and hoisted it up in the air. We were all pretty tired by then so we called it a night. Irvin went in his house to go to sleep and Dad, Jimmy, and I went home.

TWO ❧

I woke up early the next morning in my bedroom to the smell of the wood stove. I sat up on the edge of the bed and stretched my arms, grabbed my jeans and red flannel shirt from the floor, then went upstairs into the kitchen where I made some toast with peanut butter on it. I pulled up my engineer boots and went out the door, eating on the way. It was chilly out; I could see my breath.

As I walked out on the driveway, a chipmunk ran across and stopped, so I threw a piece of toast at it, then I started walking up the side of the road to Irvin's house. I would walk a little, then run, then walk. There were a lot of mail boxes on the way so I decided to flip up all the flags on them as I walked by. Some of the mailboxes had newspaper holders under them so I thought I should bring my friend a paper. I crossed over to the left side of the street, walked a couple of blocks and passed Fred and Joey's house—they were Irvin's nephews. Then I made a left up Irvin's road, or so I called it. It was a dirt road with lots of gravel.

Over on the right, about a block up, was the "Old Folks' Home" with a long stone wall out front. As I passed there was an elderly man sitting on the end, hunched over with his cane. I said "Hi," and he said, "Hi." A little further up on the same side was a huge apple tree with the best apples ever. I picked three and started eating one, then put the other two in my pockets.
I went another half a block, and still on the same side, was a field of corn—pretty big one, too.

When I went by the cornfield, there was Irvin's driveway, long and about two car lengths wide. On the left side of the driveway was the old white farmhouse surrounded by tall pines. Going further, I saw the bear hanging from the tractor next to the apple tree. In the daylight I could see just how much blood there was—kind of scary to think of the damage a twelve-gauge slug can do.

As I walked towards the house I could see Irvin through the kitchen window cooking something. I went inside. The place smelled deliciously of bacon, eggs, toast, and fresh coffee.

"Hi, Jeff," Irvin said, "Are you ready to skin the bear?"

"Yeah," I replied.

I put the newspaper on the table and told him I picked it up on the way over. "Thanks," he said, "Want some breakfast? I was just going to eat." "No, thanks," I answered back. So we sat at the table. He ate and I had a cup of coffee with sugar and milk in it. After Irvin finished eating, he sighed, stood up and yawned, walked over to the kitchen sink and put his dishes in it. We went outside, the air was still cool. I could hear a crow in the distance.

Irvin put on his railroad cap, straightened it out and we walked towards the tractor. I looked at the bear and told Irvin I wasn't up to skinning it. He laughed and said, "I kinda had a feeling you were gonna change your mind." I laughed, too. Then he said, "Well, let's bury it then."

So Irvin went in front of the old Allis Chalmers, turned it over with the hand crank and the old tractor sputtered, fired up and came to life. He walked around, climbed up onto the steel seat that was polished from years of pants rubbing on it. He put it in gear and started across the field towards a row of willow trees. I followed. The old Allis was chugging across the field in low gear, black smoke coming from the exhaust pipe. The engine was probably burning oil because it was so old.

After reaching the other side of the field, Irvin lowered the bucket of the tractor and lowered the bear to the ground. It lay there with its tongue hanging out the side of its open mouth as he unhooked the chain. Irvin got back on the tractor, backed up and scooped out a hole in the soft earth with the bucket. When it was deep enough, we rolled the bear into the hole and covered the top with dirt. It was then that I remembered the two apples I saved. I took them out of my pocket and we each ate one, leaving the bear to rest under the willow trees.

THREE

I saw the old .22 rifle leaning against the garage wall, just sitting there with beer bottles and cans piled up around it. I walked over to take a closer look; the gun was covered with dust and cobwebs. So I picked it up, brushing the stuff off and noticed somebody had spray painted the stock orange. The barrel, along with the action, were covered with surface rust, also there was no trigger guard.

I thought this would be easy to fix up, so I asked the fat, bald man standing over by the garage sale sign how much he wanted for it. "Eight bucks," he said. I had five in my pocket at the time and asked if he would take that. "Well, that gun has seen better days. I guess five sounds reasonable," he replied, scratching his double chin. Walking over, I reached in my pants pocket and took out three crumpled ones and eight quarters, handed the money over and thanked him. "You bet," he said. Then I turned around and headed for home, about two miles away.

It was around noon then, really hot outside, one of those muggy humid days in the middle of August, the kind of weather that makes your clothes stick to your body. About half way home, I had to stop and take off my jean jacket to cool off, as I did I wiped the sweat off my face with the soft denim material. It was then that I realized the rifle should be covered up so I did so with my jacket. I was almost home and walking fast, just a couple more blocks to go in this heat. Finally, I was there. The shade from the tall maple trees felt so good and cool as I entered the driveway.

I sat down in the shade for a few minutes to catch my breath, then got up and went through the front door which was already open, straight through the living room and into the kitchen, where I drank a huge glass of cold water. The house was quiet. I laid the rifle and jacket on the counter-top and made a peanut butter and jelly sandwich. Looking out the window, I could see Mom and Dad working in the garden. Dad was tilling and Mom was weeding.

I finished my sandwich, grabbed the rifle and jacket then went downstairs into the coolness of the basement, tossing the jean jacket on my bed as I walked by. Then I went into the room where the old workbench was. With my appetite and thirst taken care of I could hardly wait to take the gun apart.

I sat in the fold-out steel chair with my old beat up toolbox on the floor next to me. I reached down, picked out a screwdriver and removed the barrel, setting it on the workbench.

I had a few hours to work on the stock before supper so I took some rough sandpaper from the drawer and began to remove all the orange paint that covered it. Then after a few minutes of sanding I could see the nice wood underneath. Still anxious to see the oak grain, I didn't stop sanding until all the ugly orange paint was gone. By then, my arms were tired and my body sweaty. A couple of hours had gone by like nothing and it was still plenty hot out.

I decided to take a break and step outside the basement door for a cold drink of water and walked over to the back porch where the faucet and garden hose were, turned on the water and waited for it to run cold. I drank as much as I could and then sprayed the sweat from my face and arms.

Supper was still a few hours away. I thought I should go back into the workshop and get as much done on the stock as I could. As I was walking towards the basement door, I could see my parents were still busy in the big garden.

I went in and sat back down. Feeling refreshed from the cool water, I was ready to get started. The next step was to fine sand the stock. I took out more sandpaper and started working on it again. I couldn't believe someone could cover such a nice looking gun stock, especially with orange paint. The more I worked on it, the better the wood grain looked. Finally, I was finished sanding.

About then, I could tell Dad must have fired up the barbecue. Supper should be ready in about an hour I thought. So I went over next to the workbench and decided to start cleaning up the metal parts of the rifle. Reaching in the drawer, I found some steel wool and began scrubbing off what seemed like many years of rust and tarnish from the barrel and action. It was all coming off nicely. Underneath I could see the steel was good and shiny with no pitted spots from all the rust, just a few more minutes of rubbing down the barrel and I should be finished. Finally, I was done and it didn't take nearly as long to do as the stock did.

Whatever Dad had cooking on the grill smelled great and it was working on my appetite. I held the barrel up by the window in the sunlight to see if there were any spots I might have missed. There were none. Satisfied, I set it down and went outside. By then the whole family was outside on the patio. I walked over and sat down at the picnic table across from by brother Jim and told him about the .22 I was working on. "I want to see it," he said with curiosity. "Okay, after we eat," I said.

Dad was busy flipping burgers at the smoky grill, saying, "This should get rid of the bugs for now," as he coughed and tried to avoid the smoke. "Ya think so," Mom said smiling as she was putting down paper plates. My sisters were setting down potato salad, corn on the cob, and baked beans; all but Kristie who was only 2 years old and in her high chair drinking grape juice.

When Dad was ready, he brought the plate of grilled hamburgers over and put them on the table. Everything looked and smelled delicious. The corn was from our own garden that my family and I planted. "I can't wait to taste the corn," Sherry and Annette said at the same time, laughing. "All of us have been waiting," Jackie said with a smile.

But before everyone was to eat, Dad said he should pray first, and it went like this: "In the name of the Father, Son and Holy Ghost, the first one at the table gets the most!" "Dear," Mom said, joking back, "that's not a good example for the kids!" Jimmy and I looked at each other and smiled, while Dad did it over the right way.

As usual, everyone was quiet while we were eating. Feeling too full to eat any more I was anxious to show my brother what I had been working on. We both thanked Mom and Dad for supper, telling them it was good.

Then we went into the basement where I showed Jimmy what I was doing with the rifle. "Cool, this will look nice when it's done," he said. "Where did you find this?" he asked, as he picked up the stock and barrel, looking at them both. "I picked it up at a garage sale for five bucks," I told him. Then with my belly full of good food and feeling tired from the heat of the day, I walked over, flopped onto my bed and went to sleep.

FOUR

Up north it seems that summer turns to fall almost overnight as the days get shorter and darkness comes early. It was almost dusk. Looking out the dining room window, I could see many birds in the mountain ash tree eating at its ripe, orange, plump berries. All of a sudden, a partridge landed on the top of the tree, looked around cautiously, then ate a few berries and took off into the woods. This reminded me that hunting season was here, and I wanted to use the .22 rifle that I had finished.

Remembering the partridge last evening got me in the hunting mood. I took the .22 from the rack and went into the backyard, along with a couple of mason jars that I grabbed from the canning room. I set them on the ground and walked away, about 20 feet, thinking, "That's about the size of a partridge or rabbit."

With that in mind, I opened the bolt, put in a shell that I took from my pocket, slid the bolt forward and closed it. As I put the rifle to my shoulder, it fit perfect. Aiming for the center of the jars, I fired. Bull's-eye! I hit my mark and the glass shattered, surprisingly, without adjusting the sights. Taking out another shell, I loaded again, aimed and fired—dead on! I was all set.

It was mid-morning and the fall air was crisp. The sun was beginning to melt the frost on the ground, and the musty smell of dead leaves was in the air. It was a perfect day for the hunt.

Ahead of me was the trail, surrounded by oaks and maples, with their leaves changing from green to bright orange and yellow. I walked past and went deeper into the woods, towards the cedar swamp where there were always small game hiding out. I went further down the beaten trail, crossed the creek, and went into the marshy swamp. There was deadfall everywhere. Stepping over, my foot snapped a branch on the ground, spooking a huge buck. He looked at me and bolted, crashing through the underbrush and disappeared. After catching my breath, I went on.

The woods were dead silent except for the sounds of chickadees fluttering nearby. Walking slowly, I checked the underbrush and trees for anything hiding in them. I decided to cut across the cedar grove and hit the main trail, where I knew there were usually partridge. It was rough going with all the brush and small trees. Up ahead I saw a clearing and thought that would be easier to walk through. Still walking slowly, I started towards it.

On the other side lay an old rotting log, hollow, covered in green moss. I took a few steps more, when all of a sudden, out from the log jumped a cottontail! It was full-grown and stood there frozen, with its ears twitching like radar. Thump, thump…Thump, thump… I could hear my heart! It was just the rabbit and me. He was breathing rapidly and ready to run. I had to take the shot. Taking the safety off, I raised the rifle slowly, took aim behind the shoulder and squeezed the trigger. The shot rang out, hitting its mark! Kicking briefly, the cottontail laid still. I picked it up by its hind legs and started home.

The pond with a beaver dam.

FIVE 🐾

Some of my favorite stories were those of survival, westerns—about hardships in life. It was a quiet evening. My family and I had just finished our supper of fried chicken, mashed potatoes with gravy, and sweet peas. Again, the kitchen was warm and inviting with the smell of good cooking, along with the slight odor of the woodstove, rumbling in the basement below. Which reminded me there was firewood that needed to be brought in.

Thanking Mom for supper, I put my dishes in the sink, grabbed my jacket, and went outside into the brisk fall air. In the backyard there was the pile of firewood that Dad had sawed with his McCulloch chain saw and I had split with a steel wedge and sledgehammer Irvin had lent to us.

The sky was a light blue with a pinkish glow to it as the sun settled. Just enough daylight left to get some work done, and then it would soon be dark. Next to the tin shed laid a wooden toboggan. There was no snow on the ground yet, but I had an idea. I went over, setting it next to the woodpile and began stacking the split pieces on top of the old sled, one by one, until there was a good amount. Then taking the rope, which was tied to the front, I began pulling it up the hill towards the house. The going was a little tough, but it sure beat making so many trips back and forth one armful at a time.

After seven sleds full, I decided to do one more to make it eight. I just liked even numbers, I guess. After stacking the firewood neatly against a basement wall, I was satisfied that I got more done than usual, just by using my imagination. I brought the toboggan back outside.

The floor was pretty messy after I was done. Next thing I knew, Mom was sweeping up all the little pieces of bark, wood-chips and mud.

"Looks like you got a lot done. Thanks," she said, while sweeping the mess onto a dustpan and into a garbage bag.

"Yea," I said back. Tired from the chore, I took off my jacket, set it on the backrest of a chair in my room and went upstairs.

Dad was sitting in his recliner, reading the newspaper. Jimmy and my sisters were going about their own business. Sweaty, I went into the bathroom and let the faucet run hot. The water felt soothing as I washed my hands and face. As I was drying off, I smelled popcorn. Dad was in the kitchen trying out his new hot air popper. "There's a good movie on tonight."

"What is it?" I asked. "Jeremiah Johnson—it's about a guy who goes up into the mountains, living as a hunter and trapper. It's gonna be good," he said.

Well, it turned out the movie was very good and filled my head full of ideas, which led me to my next adventure.

It was a restless night, to say the least. In the movie, Jeremiah Johnson had to build a log cabin. It took place in the mountains and sent my imagination soaring.

While I was hunting in the woods down in the swampy marsh a while ago, I discovered a special place where there was a ridge surrounded by tall poplar, pine, and cedar trees. On its right was a huge pond, the size of a small lake, that the beavers made by building their dam over a good sized creek.

On the left was a smaller pond where water collected just because the land was lower in that area. It was still and stagnant, giving off a strong swampy odor, unlike its bigger brother. What a perfect place to put up a fort, I thought, while cracking open a couple of hard boiled eggs for breakfast. It was a weekend and I was the first one up, ready to start the day.

The woods were a very good size and along its outer edges were four roads which border-lined the whole area through our backyard and onto the trails. I could reach all the good junk piles the neighbors had in their backyards. It would be like a hidden treasure—you never knew what you would find. After eating the eggs, I drank a nice cold glass of grape juice to top off the simple meal and headed out. Well, after a few hours of sheer will and determination, I gathered up a bunch of used lumber and a half a roll of tar paper that appeared to have sat outside for quite some time but would still work out just fine. It took a lot of work and sweat, but I hauled all of it to the edge of the smaller pond, which was still nice in its own special way and closer to home.

By now the chill of the cold morning had left and the warm autumn sun beat down, bringing the woods back to life. The leaves on the trees with their warm colors looked like they were glowing as the rays shone through them. I could hear the many different birds singing their songs happily and eating the many different wild berries and the occasional sound of a woodpecker tapping on the trees, trying to make a meal from the insects inside them. The squirrels, too, were out gathering acorns. They all sensed the long cold winter was on its way and feasted on the bountiful fall harvest, which reminded me I should get home and eat lunch.

Walking back up hill and towards the backyard, I could hear the sound of Dad's tiller turning up soil in the now barren garden. A little further ahead I could see the many rows of freshly tilled dirt and the robins picking earthworms that the turning blades brought to the surface. Up the porch and into the kitchen, I looked in the cupboards for something to eat. Digging through, I found a tin of sardines and some soda crackers—perfect! Then I went down into the basement where I got a saw and hammer from the old workbench. With food and tools I was set and headed back towards the swampy bog.

Past the garden and big oak tree, I went down the steep hill, crossing a small creek on a log I had put across weeks before. This was kind of like a secret passage. Once across I worked my way through the narrow trail to my hidden domain. Finally there, I sat down on a tree trunk that lay on its side, probably from the high winds during spring. After hanging the saw and hammer on a branch, I peeled open the tin of sardines. Since I had no fork I scooped them out one at a time with the soda crackers and ate them. With my belly full, I put the leftover crackers on the tree trunk, walked over and sorted through the various pieces of lumber. After taking out the longest boards, I grabbed the hammer from the branch and began pulling out the bent nails one by one until the wood was clean.

Right on the edge of the small pond were four cedar trees growing in a square pattern about six feet apart from each other. This would be the best spot in the area to build the shack. Since there were a lot of big black bears in the woods, I thought I would put the floor close to the ground and have the smallest doorway possible underneath. That way, if a bear did come along, the beast would have a hard time getting in and I would be safe in my shelter.

Next to the fallen tree where I had hung the saw and hammer lay a good-sized rock, half buried, with a flat, smooth surface on top, slightly covered with green moss—just what I needed. I gathered up the oddly bent nails I had pulled from the lumber, setting them on the ground next to the rock. Then, taking the claws of the hammer, which are used for pulling out nails, I scraped off what moss there was on the stone's flat surface. Since I had no nails at home, I took each nail and tapped them as straight as I could on my newfound workbench. With the lumber stripped clean and the nails straightened, I was ready to start building my secret getaway.

There were many branches on the four cedar trees, most of them in the way and needed to be trimmed. Taking the saw from the branch it was hanging on, I decided to cut them from the tree's trunk. I started from the bottom, working my way up. With every back and forth stroke, the saw blade cut deeper into the branches, filling my nostrils with the rich smell of freshly cut cedar; a refreshing change from the stagnant odor of the small pond.

Taking out the best pieces of lumber so the floor would be good and strong, I started on the framework. Two feet off the ground should be good—just enough room to crawl up and in, and low enough to keep anything large out. It went up fairly easily and the doorway was not too big and not too small—just right. All I needed now was something to make the floor's surface. Right then I had a great idea—up by the tin shed lay a stack of plywood, the sheets of wood were from an ice fishing house that was no longer in use but they would suit me just fine.

After stacking two sheets on top of each other and dragging them down through the woods, I was there. Everything was good except for a couple of slivers that stuck in my hand. They were deep, so with the aid of tweezers from my Swiss army knife, I pulled them out. Then I laid the plywood next to each other across the floor frame and sat down. What a great view! The spot was slightly uphill and overlooked the small pond, now reflecting the bright sun like a mirror. I just had to sit a while and take it all in.

After ten minutes or so, I lined up the plywood then nailed it down; only this time with new nails I found in the workbench. With the branches cleared and the floor up, it looked great!

Six

I was in my bedroom, taking a break but still thinking about the shack. Above the woodstove, in groups of five, were twenty small No. 2 traps hanging from a beam by their chains. In the corners were two bows and a quiver full of arrows, snowshoes, and fishing gear—with my guns on the wall, I felt very content. My room had everything I needed to escape to the outdoors.

As I lay there on my bed, daydreaming, I remembered something and got up. This would be a good night to have a campfire and a cookout, and I knew just what was on the menu. On the row of firewood was a box of wooden matches—the kind you could strike anywhere. I grabbed a few and put them in my pocket, then went upstairs into the kitchen.

There were many different spices as I opened a small drawer next to the cook stove and looked in. Not knowing much about the stuff, I fumbled through the little boxes and tins, trying to figure out what to use. Setting out the usual salt and pepper on the butcher block then looked some more—nutmeg, cloves, ginger—I smelled all three. It was nice but I didn't think they would go well with my dish. Hmmmmm— seasoned salt, garlic powder, and red pepper—this was more like it. Not measuring, I put a little of each in a small sandwich bag, then walked over to the fridge. In the freezer above, I took out the rabbit I had harvested from the hollow log. All I needed now was something to cook the critter in.

Looking through the cupboards below, I found a copper kettle. With this I could make soup, and if I were going to do that, vegetables were in need. I opened the refrigerator door—bingo! Inside were carrots, potatoes, onions, and celery—just what the doctor ordered. I took what I needed, then put everything in a garbage bag. The festivities were about to begin.

Thinking about the soup I was about to make brought me back to my soon-to-be shack in no time. The woods were still and quiet except for the sound of squirrels rustling about in the fallen leaves.

Anxious to get started, I set the bag down on a flat part of the ground and began clearing a spot for the campfire. There were plenty of small branches and twigs lying around. I gathered some up for kindling, breaking the thicker stuff across my knee. When I thought there was enough, I tore some tarpaper from the roll, crumpling it up. That should get things going, I thought. Then, carefully, I stacked the kindling on top—first the small twigs then larger pieces over them. Darkness was setting in fast. Grabbing the matches from my pocket, I struck one on a nearby rock—it lit. I waited for it to get going a little better then held the flame under the tarpaper—it began to burn in no time and the kindling was soon a blaze.

I broke up and added more wood to the fire. It was burning good enough on its own now, so I went around the site picking up and made a small pile—just enough for a couple of hours. With the fire crackling and sending sparks into the night sky, I felt good—like nothing else mattered. I found a nice log that I laid next to my woodpile. There. I could reach over and stoke up the fire as needed without getting up. Now I could prepare supper.

Reaching over I took the copper kettle and rabbit from the bag. By now the fire burned down some, making some nice coals. Placing the rabbit into the kettle and adding some water I brought with, I set it next to the fire to simmer.

As I took the vegetables from the bag, something just crossed my mind—this time of year, bears are trying to fatten up before hibernation. What if one smells the soup and comes prowling around? That could be a bad situation, but then I thought the fire would keep any creatures of the night a safe distance from me. So with my trusty Swiss army knife, I started cutting up the vegetables, piece by piece, tossing them in the pot and put the thought of the bear out of my mind. The water was now at a good boil. Just one more thing—the spices—I added them to the mixture and waited patiently.

I sat there, staring into the reddish white coals, feeling their warmth, getting lost, no worries, thinking about nothing—just enjoying. And with the smell of the soup cooking, there was no other place I'd rather be. It wasn't much longer I pulled the soup away from the fire, letting it cool off. After a little while, I took a taste – it was delicious! I ate 'til I was full, savoring the warm spicy broth, then put the rest of the wood on the fire and lay beside it.

SEVEN

It was twenty minutes before closing and shopping hours were coming to an end as dad and I entered the department store and headed towards the sporting goods section. There weren't many people and this time of year the stores felt like home to me, especially the sight of ice fishing tip-ups, augers, fish spears, and winter wear. On one of the shelves I noticed a silver hand warmer, the kind that looks like an oversized cigarette lighter. Along side it lay a red felt bag with a yellow string. I sure would like one of these I thought.

Dad was looking at a pair of leather choppers and grabbed them. "Let's go before they close," he said. Next to the checkout counter was a big glass display case and in it were fishing reels, gun scopes, hunting knives, and handguns. Behind on the wall, standing upright, were shotguns, rifles, fishing poles, and archery supplies.

"How's it going tonight?" the salesman asked me.

"Pretty good. Do you have any shotgun slugs?"

"Sure we do – what kind do ya need?"

"20-guage," I replied.

"Well, let's see here. Ahh, here we go, I've got Federal and Winchester. They come in boxes of five—what's your taste?"

"I'll take one of each."

"Anything else?"

"Yeah, a couple big game licenses and two boxes of 180 grain 30.06," Dad answered as he set the gloves down and pulled out his wallet.

"Remington's all we have," said the salesman.

"I'll take two boxes. They'll do the job," said Dad.

"They sure will. I just need your John Hancock," the salesman said while setting two big game licenses and tags on the counter and ringing everything up.

It was early morning; everything was quiet for the most part, except the sound of Dad's new Dodge with its six-cylinder engine warming up in the driveway. I had just gotten dressed in my red deer hunting clothes, slid the 20-guage pump in its case and set it on the kitchen table. In a hurry, I had some toast and coffee. Dad already had eaten breakfast and was putting on his boots. "Get the guns and put them in the car so we can head out. We might do some bird hunting later so I set the 12-guage next to the deer rifle," he said.

With that in my mind, I went back down into the bedroom, opened the desk drawer and put the two boxes of slugs along with a few shotgun shells into my pockets. Visions of big bucks, bear, and small game went through my head as I picked up the guns from the workbench and put them in their cases. I went upstairs and into the kitchen. Mom was up and opened the door, "Be careful hunting today."

"I will," I answered back then stepped outside. It was one of those foggy fall mornings when you didn't know if it would start to rain or the sun would shine.

Still dark out, I stepped down the porch with one case in each hand and walked toward the running car. I kinda liked the smell of its exhaust mixed with the cool damp air outside. When I opened the back door, I noticed there was a windshield ice scraper with its wooden handle propped against the gas pedal and steering column. Dad put it there to keep the engine revved. I laid the two guns down on the back seat and as I was walking back toward the house to get my 20-guage, I heard the car's door slam shut. Then all of a sudden the rear tires chirped and she took off right down a steep embankment – guns and all – smashing head on into a huge yellow birch tree, which stopped it dead in her tracks! In no time at all Dad came out the back door, "What the Sam heck is going on?!" he shouted while running over and down the hill to shut the car's engine off.

"Darn it all to heck! Now I'll have to call a wrecker to pull the darn thing out! What the heck happened?"

"I don't know, I just looked and the next thing I knew it was in the Ditch!"

"Ahhhh, we'll take your ma's car then. Get the guns. I'm gonna grab my thermos."

Then out came Mom, "Is everything alright?"

"Yeah, I'll take care of it later. Right now John's waiting on us."

I put the guns in the back of the Ford station wagon and sat in the front seat, waiting while Dad said 'bye' to Mom.

It was about three miles before our destination, still slightly foggy out as the headlights shone ahead. Then suddenly across the road leaped two does and a giant buck.

"Look! Must be a ten –pointer!" Dad shouted.

"Yeah it does! I can't wait to get out and hunt!" I said, excitedly.

"We're almost there, then we'll check out the power line that goes through the woods," answered Dad.

Soon, we pulled into John's driveway. The yellowish porch light shone through the foggy darkness as Dad went up and knocked on the door. Next to a long garage I noticed a race car made for a dirt track. It looked fast just sitting there sporting its number '56' on the door and wide tires. I had to get out and take a look! I just loved it! Inside was a roll cage. In front of the driver's seat where the window used to be, a heavy steel screen was in its place to keep out any flying debris and on the dash a tachometer with its redline to watch the engines RPM's. I was lost in a daydream, racing around a muddy track when I heard a voice.

It was John, "How would you like to drive a car like that?"

"I'd love to! Maybe some day," I answered back.

"Yeah, I'm going to build another one this winter—a late model. It's going to be a real rocket ship!"

"Hey Hondo! Whataya think?" Dad asked me.

"Pretty cool."

"Well, we're burning daylight. We should head out. What are you shooting today?" John asked.

"Jeff's got my old 20-guage and I have a 30.06 Mauser his Uncle Tommy gave me while we visited in Montana. Here, I'll show ya." Dad pulled the rifle from its case, "There's no bolt! Where's the bolt?"

I remembered putting the gun in the case and the bolt was missing but I thought nothing of it. Maybe Dad placed it in his jacket pocket and forgot it. Oh well, it was gone.

"Darn it! We gotta run back to the house and get it!"

"Okay, okay... I'll just do something around here 'til you get back," John said.

Making it home in half the time it took to get to John's, I waited in the car while Dad went in the house and got the bolt. I don't think two words were said the whole way. In a year from now none of this is going to matter and it will be forgotten. Maybe if we get home early enough I can spend some time working on my shack, I thought.

"I just talked to John. He's going to meet us on the hunting trail. We can still get a good start," Dad said. Things were starting to lighten up.

"Okay," I replied.

Then off we sped, quickly reaching our hunting area in no time. I could see John's car parked off to the side as we pulled in. "Hey, Lou, there's a spot on top of the power line. We'll be able to see the whole area if we go there."

"Sounds good," Dad whispered back.

Taking out my 20-guage, I loaded it with Federals. It was cold out, but not enough to wear gloves. By now the sun had just peeked over the horizon and the fog was starting to burn off. We walked slowly without saying a word, avoiding puddles of water that formed in the lower parts of the trail.

Ahead I could see the power line with its cable-like wires towering above. "There's a good place to sit. The grass is tall so the deer won't see us," John whispered. Each of us found a spot about twenty feet apart from each other. With the whole width of the power line covered, we waited.

There was no movement and a good hour had gone by when Dad motioned to walk ahead. All three of us went quite a distance, taking our time and being quiet as possible. Suddenly on Dad's side a big buck leaped out about 75 yards down. Raising the Mauser quickly, he fired. It was loud—almost thunder like—echoing through the valley.

"Did ya get 'em?" John yelled.

"I'm not sure, I'll go see if there's any sign." Going to the site, Dad shouted, "Yeah! There's blood and hair!"

"Really? You must have got 'em good!"

"Nah, just kidding ya," Dad said jokingly back to John.

"Well that sounded like a cannon going off. I'm sure all the deer are gone from here."

A while later, we were back at the car. Dad took out his thermos, the hot coffee smelled so good as he filled the cup. "Here, drink some," he said, and I did.

"Well, what are your plans, Lou?"

"Might hunt a little more. How about you?"

"I've got a few projects going on at home I should tend to," answered John.

By now it was midday, the sun was shining and it was warmer than usual outside. John left for home. We were driving down a bumpy road full of potholes, heading deeper into the countryside, when Dad noticed a small bait shop and pulled in. "I'm gonna get a couple things. I'll be back in a few minutes," he said. I fumbled with the radio while he was inside. With nothing good to listen to, I shut it off. What's taking him so long I thought. Finally the front door opened on the shop and out came Dad, carrying a small paper bag.

He got into the car, "Yeah, I just ran into an old buddy and we started 'bs'ing. Here I got us some jerky and sunflower seeds."

"Where should we go now?" I asked.

"I got a cool place we can go to."

"Where?"

"You'll see," he said.

I chewed on some beef jerky and said no more. Sometime later we were on a long stretch of road with many high and low spots. Up and down the car went just like a roller coaster.

On one side of the road there was an apple orchard surrounded by a fence. Further ahead on the right side, was a gravel road. We turned and went onward, "Not too much further," Dad said while spitting sunflower shells out the window. Looking out my side, I saw a gravel pit with front-end loaders and dump trucks driving around, and a long conveyer belt dumping small rocks into a pile. The sun shone through the windshield, blinding my view. Reaching up, I pulled the visor down. It was then I saw a small brown pony in a pasture and behind it, a red barn. "We're here," said Dad. The garage door was open and we got out of the old Ford and walked toward it.

There stood Uncle Mike, working on a chainsaw, "Hey dago! How's it going?"

"Hey! Not bad, not bad."

"I'm just changing the spark plug on the saw so I can clean some dead trees around here. How's yourself?"

"Just wondering if you're up to some bird hunting?" Dad asked, "Sure seems like a good day for it." Dad looked at the spark plug, "She's running a little rich, it's all carboned up."

"Yeah, I guess it is at that," Mike said as he flipped up the clip-on shades for his glasses. "How ya doin' Jeff? Ready to get some partridge? Your mom's a good cook—she'll find something to do with 'em. Just the other day I came home from work and there were two partridges behind the garage. So, I hurried into the house, got the 22/20 gauge and shot both. That's what was for supper that evening."

"How'd ya cook 'em?"

"Just fried 'em up," he told me while tightening the new spark plug.

"I never heard of that kind of gun."

"I'll show you in a little bit here."

"Where's the family?"

"The wife's visiting her parents and Jimmy's down the road trout fishing," he told Dad.

"Trout fishing?"

"Yeah, there's brook trout in the creek by the gravel pit. Jimmy goes there once a week. They're good fried up, too."

"There's a place up the road we could try, let me wash up and I'll be back in a few."

"All-righty, we'll wait out here," Dad told Mike. With that said, I could hardly wait. Soon, with our shotguns loaded and in hand, Mike came out, "Hey, ya gotta see this. I can shoot a shotgun or 22-shell," he said while loading his shotgun rifle combination. "See the switch here on the hammer? Ya just flip it to which barrel you want to fire first. I can get rabbits with the .22 and birds with the shotgun."

Cool! Some day I'd like to have one of those 'two guns in one' I thought. "Cool! I never knew they made 'em like that," said Dad. We left the driveway and were up the road a ways, "See the swamp over here? A couple of weeks ago I saw a big moose walking down in there. Yeah, it surprised the heck outta me!"

"Some day you'll have to get a moose license," Dad said back.

"Yeah really. I could feed the family a good couple years at that. Sure would save a lot on the grocery bill, right?" Then Mike raised his gun and stopped. "Ahhhh!"

"What is it?"

"Darn flickertail woodpecker, they look just like a partridge," Mike told Dad.

After the false alarm, we walked quieter, focusing more on the hunt. "Ahh! There's one!" Looking ahead I could see a partridge basking on a sunny spot. It fluttered its feathers and started walking fast, and then flapping its wings, it burst into flight. Dad fired, hitting the bird. It fell from the sky and landed in a wooded area below. "Great shot!" yelled Mike. I went over and started looking for the bird. There it was, hardly noticeable, blending in perfectly on the forest floor. I picked it up and we went back to Mike's farm.

"A few days ago I drove the Harley up here. Look, there's still tire tracks on the trail."

"Harley?" I asked.

"Yeah, I picked one up early this spring, got a good deal too. The transmission wasn't shifting into gear like it should so the guy let it go for a good price."

"Cool! Can we take a look at it?" I asked Mike.

"Yeah, I think I can manage that."

"What about the transmission?" asked Dad.

"It's working fine now, had it rebuilt. Maybe I'll fire it up."
Cool, I can't wait, I thought. Soon we were at the end of the trail and crossed the road into Mike's driveway. I put the guns in the car while Dad and Mike went inside the house. When I closed the door and turned, to my surprise, there was my cousin Jimmy, with his fishing pole and three brook trout on a stringer.

"Hi Jeff," he said, grinning from ear to ear. "Look what I caught!"

"I see that. You'll have to show me the creek sometime. Man, I'd love to catch some of them."

"I will. How long are you gonna stay?"

"I'm not sure, we'll see what Dad says," I said. "Looks like ya got a haircut."

"Yeah, Mom cuts it pretty close."

"Yeah she did. Man, that's short!" I told him. Dad and Mike came out,

"Hey, Jimmy, ya caught a few trout—alright! Alright!" Mike said proudly. He then walked over to a plywood shed and took out a set of keys, removed the padlock and opened the two doors. There it was—a 350 Harley Davidson Sprint, maroon with a black seat! Flipping up the kickstand, Mike pushed it out onto the driveway. He turned the key and kicked it over. The engine fired and ran smooth the first try. "Hey, Lou, whattya think?" Mike shouted as he twisted the throttle back and forth, revving the engine. Dad gave him the 'thumbs up' sign, and he sped off down the driveway and up the gravelly road. First…second… third…fourth…it shifted through the gears perfectly.

"Do you think he'll let me drive it?" I asked Jimmy.

"Maybe," he said with that smile back on his face.

Dad stood at the end of the driveway looking for Mike. I could hear the Harley slow down. "He must be turning around—here he comes," said Dad. The distant sound of its engine grew louder.

Suddenly, there he was, "It's running great! Give it a shot!"

"I've been waiting, too," Dad said excitedly. They traded places. Revving it up, Dad leaned forward. "This is how ya take off when racing flat track!" Holding the gas wide open, he popped the clutch and was gone, leaving spit up gravel behind. Mike was laughing hard.

"That was good! Would it be okay if I took it for a ride?"

"Well, if your dad says it's alright, you can. Just then Dad came down the hill and pulled up.

"Hey! Ya gotta do that again!"

"Do what?" Dad asked while wiping his eyes.

"Take off again like you're going to race!"

Again Dad revved up the bike, dumping the clutch. Mike was

laughing again with his arms crossed. I could tell he got a kick out of it. Dad was back again, "Jeff wants to give it a try," said Mike.

"Do ya think you can handle it?"

"Yeah, I can."

"It's pretty heavy, don't say I didn't warn you."

It was my turn – I revved 'er up!

"The faster ya go, the easier it is. When you turn around up there, don't slow down too much or you'll dump it—ya got it?" Dad asked.

"Yep." Not knowing the bike's power I eased up on the clutch then took off. As I put on the gas, the front lifted with every shift but not enough to pull a wheelie. I was coming up to the end of the road when I remembered Dad's words. Keeping the speed up, I turned around just fine then headed back downhill. Feeling more confident, I gave 'er more gas than before. The rear tire spun, putting the bike a little sideways. I let off and it straightened itself. In no time I was back. "Good job!" Dad said, "I'm going to park it."

"Yeah, ya did good Jeff. Pretty fun, huh?" Mike asked.

It was late afternoon and getting cold out. "Why don't you take the partridge?"

"You sure?"

"Yeah, it's getting late. We need to head out."

"Hey, thanks, man. I think I'll fry it up with the brook trout for supper," Mike told Dad.

It turned out to be a good day after all, even though Dad missed the buck and the car went in the ditch. On the way home I was tired and fell asleep, dreaming about my shack.

EIGHT 🌿

It was cloudy and gray as snowflakes gently fell covering the backyard with a fresh white blanket. I had just brought the last piece of plywood down from the shed setting it next to the shack floor. There were five left. That should be enough to finish off the walls and roof,

I thought. All I needed to do now was find my tools so I could get to work. Where could they be hiding under this snow? I had no idea. Right then I remembered the fallen tree and walked toward it. There they were, the saw and hammer hanging from the branch where I had left them. The shack floor had a few inches of snow built up so I brushed it off. Underneath I found the rest of the nails still in their box. After setting the tools down beside them I looked around. Both ponds had a thin crust of ice forming around the edges. If I was going to feel comfortable and warm, a fire was needed.

Nearby there were many poplar trees, most of them from waist high to the top were full of dead branches. Perfect for getting a fire started. I went from tree to tree, breaking off different sizes of the gray, dried out wood. Soon I had a bundle in my arms. Walking over to where I had the campfire a few days ago, I kicked away the little snow that was there. I put a match to the bone-dry kindling and in no time it was snapping and popping, filling the air with that great smoky smell.

I looked at the plywood… hmmmm… this is going to be easy. It was about the same length as the trees were apart. Taking one of the sheets, I rested the bottom edge on the floor and put a nail through each top corner to hold it in place. I hammered in six more nails on each side, anchoring the sheet of wood to the tree's trunk. The next two walls went up fairly quick, leaving the front side open, facing the fire.

By now it had quit snowing. Rather than finishing the front wall, I thought it would be easier to put the roof on now. My hands were cold. I warmed them next to the fire and stacked on some more poplar branches to the dying flames. With my hands warm, I laid a piece of plywood over the top. It fit just about perfectly. I didn't even nail it down. Its own weight would keep it in place. I took a break and could feel the fire's warmth reflecting off the inside of the walls as I sat on the open edge.

Suddenly I had an idea, behind the oak tree was a small scrap pile. If I remembered right, there was some stovepipe lying around. I jumped up, kicked some snow on the fire and went to check it out. I was anxious, hurrying, just a hop, skip and a jump and soon I was there. I stood there looking around—everything was covered with a little snow.

I know it's here somewhere. I went to the other side through the dried up brown waist-high grass. Alright! There it was, half covered. There were a couple of pieces, one had an elbow that would work out, but the rest was rusty and full of holes. The other was in good condition and just about the right length. On top of the scrap pile, was a canister of some sort, about the size of a large coffee can. It had a short neck and lid on top. This is going to work out great. I pulled the dead grass from the good pieces of pipe and set them on the trail. My hands were getting cold. It was then I tucked the metal canister under an arm and headed for the workbench.

I knew just what I was going to do and closed the basement door behind me. I grabbed a pair of tin snips from a shelf and cut about a six by six inch square hole on one side of the container. That should do it. I stepped outside and back down the hill, feeling good because things were going well. That's when I heard the sound of a snowmobile hitting the trail. Whoever it was, I could see that familiar yellow color with black stripes through the now leafless trees below.

It's kinda funny how some people get that urge to take out their sleds with hardly any snow on the ground. I've even seen snowmobile tracks all over back there in the middle of summer. I guess you could call it the 'winter bug.' Somehow ya get that way, living in Northern Minnesota.

Well, back to business. I grabbed the two pieces of good stovepipe. My hands were full, carrying the canister and all. I finally got there and went right to work.

The ground wasn't quite frozen yet; just loose enough to pry out the flat stone I was using for a workbench. It was about three inches thick and oblong. I got it out of the ground and placed it on the shack floor. The last piece of plywood was a little water damaged from sitting on the ground too long but that was no problem. I found a spot where the wood was soft and took the heel of my engineer boots and stomped a hole where I thought the stovepipe should come through. Happy with that, I nailed it in place. Darn it! I should have put the stovepipe and canister in before I put the wall up. Oh well, I crawled through the floor and got them inside. Let's see here, I slid the stone right under the hole then set the canister on top of it with the open side facing inward. So far, so good. This was going to be cool.

After attaching the two pieces together, I pushed and twisted the stovepipe back and forth over the canister's neck. No smoke will leak from here, I thought, while placing the end out of the sidewall. On some of the boards were pieces of pink fiberglass insulation. The hole was big enough to pack it around. This way it would keep the hot, soon to be chimney, from catching the wall on fire. It got pretty chilly outside and I could hardly wait to test my miniature woodstove.

Outside I gathered some small twigs and birch bark and then scooted back in through the bear proof entry. At first I put some birch bark in the small stove and lit it. The smoke seemed to go up and through the pipe with no problems so I added some wood. It was working great. Soon the shack got toasty warm inside. I took my jacket off, lying on it next to the stove's warmth. I wish I had that bear skin rug Irvin offered me and the bear steaks to cook. This time of year, even though I built my shack with the floor lowered, the woods would be a safe place because by now the beasts should be deep in their dens hibernating for a long winter's nap. It was so peaceful and relaxing. I could understand why Jeremiah Johnson moved into the wilderness.

The boards remaining from Jeff's old fort.

NINE

It was late afternoon and freezing outside. The streets were freshly plowed and there was about a foot of snow on the ground. I took off one of the leather choppers Dad gave me and pulled the trusty Swiss Army Knife from my pant's pocket. There they were—a stack of fifty newspapers. I reached down and cut the plastic strap that bound them together. Well, I had my work cut out for the next couple of hours, I thought, while stuffing the canvas carrying bag that said *Duluth Herald* printed boldly on its side. With the sack full, I put its strap over my shoulder and headed up a steep road, known as Basswood, to deliver the town's daily news.

I went from neighbor to neighbor, setting the newspaper between their inner and outside storm door. Some people were home and gladly welcomed me. Sometimes the wonderful smell of a good home cooked meal would fill the chilled winter air as they opened the door. And, if I was lucky, someone might give me a tip of fifty cents or more. As I continued onward, I noticed quite a few snowmobiles, some on trailers and others in the front yard. Often times, at home, I would daydream and draw pictures of Ski-doos, Scorpions, Arctic Cats and other snow machines, imagining what it would be like to drive them. Here comes one now, over the top and down Basswood's steep slope, a Bombardier TNT with its yellow and black colors. It sped by leaving that smell of a two-cycle engine behind. It was getting dark out, I could see sparks flying out from under the sled's skis as it went across an open spot of pavement. Cool! Just seeing that made my paper route worth getting out.

I took a newspaper from the carrying bag and walked up the next driveway. This neighbor had a yard light on and I could see there was a snowmobile like no other, half covered with snow and on a trailer. I went back to get a closer look. It was light blue with a red seat, not the greatest looking sled but still something to have fun with. I turned and walked toward the front yard.

"How ya doin'? Pretty chilly out," the guy said while holding the front door open.

"Ooohhh, I'm doin' pretty good. I was wondering something."

"Yes, what might that be?" the man asked me.

"Well it looks like nobody's using that snowmobile. Would you sell it?"

"Hmmmmm, I think I could let it go for the right price. Why don't you step inside and we'll talk about it," he said.

"Okay."

So, up the front stairs and into the living room I went. The guy's whole family was watching TV and eating popcorn.

"Now, you were asking how much I wanted for the sled out back."

"Yeah, how much?" I asked.

"Well, what do you think it's worth?"

"I'm not sure."

"How about two hundred fifty?"

"That would take a long time to save up. My paper route doesn't pay very much."

"Hmmmm, how bad do you want it?"

"Well, it would be nice to have."

"I'll tell you what—I'll let ya take it off my hands for twenty-five dollars."

"Really?!"

"Yep, you'll have to find a way to get it home though."

"I'll find a way, thanks! I'll bring you the money tomorrow."

"Alright then, I'll be here. See ya later."

All those days of delivering papers and doing chores for the neighbors finally paid off. I forked over twenty-five dollars of my hard earned money.

"Have fun! It just needs a little tinkering and it should run. Just in case anyone should ask where you got it, show them this," and he handed me a piece of paper. I read it and felt proud! The note said, "Paid in full."

Well, like I said, it wasn't the greatest looking snowmobile but so what, it was mine—bought and paid for.

That was a few days ago. With the help of my Uncle Stewart

and his snowmobile trailer, here it was—at home, in the driveway. It was too cold out to do any work on the machine, but I planned way ahead of time. Let's see here, the basement door's about this wide and the front skis are about that far apart. No problem, I could fit the sled through here. So, with the aid of my socket set, I broke free the rusty bolts and removed the skis. Nobody was home at the time, but that suited me just fine. That way, there would be no questions of what I was doing. Ahhh, yes, the basement was warm and the snowmobile fit through its door with not an inch to spare. There should be enough space in here…yep, there was.

I had a pretty big bedroom. It was cool in the summer and warm in the wintertime. There was nothing on the opposite side of where my bed and dresser were—that would be a perfect work place. I took my jacket off and pulled the old sled in. Most of the snow was brushed off but there was just enough to leave droplets of water all over the entryway. Hmmm…there was still some ice stuck to the track. I needed to get it off the floor. What should I use? I looked around the row of firewood. There were a few pieces not split—that would work great, I thought. I grabbed three of them and put two under the front where the skis bolted on and then one in the back. It was off the floor now. Underneath I could see many dead leaves had found their way between the boagie wheels and track, which was surprisingly in almost new condition.

After cleaning out the leaves and debris, I looked the sled over. Man, this was in rough shape. The rope on the recoil was hanging out and almost worn in half. There was no linkage to hook up the throttle cable. The spark plug insulator was cracked off and the seat was torn. Not to mention the headlights, two wires weren't hooked up. It had no windshield but that wasn't a big deal. I could live without it. By now, the old machine had warmed up, forming a puddle of water underneath.

Where should I start? Well, for starters, I got my toolbox out from under the bed and opened it. I think I should take off the cowling and have a look. Half of the nuts and bolts holding it on were missing but it seemed secure enough. I grabbed my socket set, took them off and removed the snowmobile's hood, which read "Sears Snow Sled," then set it on the basement floor. Let's have a look—everything seemed to be in working order, just greasy and grimy. The drive belt was in good shape. The front pulley was still shiny and smooth inside. I then unfastened the belt guard.

The clutch looked to be in great shape too. Its surface was smooth where the belt rode, so that was all good. When I turned the front pulley, the track loosened up and moved freely. I noticed there was no gas cap either. Oh well, I'll find something to fix that. On the back of the seat was a pouch containing a tool kit. I looked inside. All it had was a spark plug wrench and two spark plugs, one used and the other still new in its cardboard container. All right! Right away, I removed the old plug. To my surprise it came out easily without much effort. The gap on the new plug seemed to be about the same as the one I took out. So, carefully, I turned it by hand and secured it into the engine's cylinder head, with a good turn of the wrench. So far, so good. I looked inside the spark plug wire's cap. It was clean and not corroded. I found a rag in the toolbox, wiped the plug wire clean and secured its cap to the plug.

What does an engine need to run? Spark to ignite the air fuel mixture and the gasoline must flow through the fuel line without any hesitation. With that in mind, I disconnected the line from the bottom of the carburetor, stretched it out straight, wiping all of the black belt dust and oil from it.

With that done, I could see the once grimy fuel line was clear in color and had no cracks or pinholes on it. Just to see if there were any obstructions, I put it in my mouth and blew into it. The air went through with no problem. There were no bubbly sounds coming from the gas tank which meant it was empty. That was good because then I wouldn't have to empty out any old gas and could put fresh stuff right in.

About now, I was feeling pretty good, having visions of hitting the trails. It was my first snowmobile and I couldn't wait to test it out. Let's see… spark, gas, oil, and air. Getting air to the engine wouldn't be a problem because there wasn't an air filter on the carburetor either. The gas line was a little loose and worn out on the end. So, I snipped about an inch of it off, and then reconnected it to the carburetor's bowl. It was a good secure fit now and should draw up fuel without air leakage.

The recoil had all of its bolts keeping it in place. I got out the right sized socket and took off the whole works. When I looked inside its shroud, I noticed the rewind spring was broken. I also could see the fly wheel had a place where a rope could be wrapped around and you could pull it over that way to start the engine. No problem! I just left the recoil off and would do it like that. The house was dead quiet except for the sounds of the wood stove crackling, when I heard the front door open upstairs. Dad and Mom were home. I grabbed a broom and swept up the dead leaves, trying to play it cool, wondering what Dad's reaction would be when he came down the stairs. I scooped up the leaves with a dustpan and put them in the garbage. There we go! It's pretty clean down here. I don't think he will get too upset.

Right then the door on top of the basement stairs opened and here he came. Time stood still for a few seconds, or so it seemed. Then I could hear the wood stove door creak as he opened it and put more wood in. The door closed and he walked towards the laundry room, where you could see right into my bedroom. Any minute now... what would be said? I waited. Then I heard, "What's going on down here? What are you doing? Your room is NOT a garage!

"I know. It's just that it's warm in here and easier to work on. Besides, I almost have it ready to fire up," I told Dad.

"Alright, but as soon as you are done, I want that thing outside. Understood?!"

"Yeah, do you have time to run me up to the gas station?"

"We'll see what your ma says. She'll probably end up having a fit when she sees what's in your room."

Right then, Mom came down the stairs, "What's this doing in your room?"

"I'm just fixing it up and then I'll bring it back outside," I explained.

"Well, okay, just don't keep it in here too long."

They both went back upstairs and I grabbed six bucks from my change jar when I heard my brother Jimmy come through the basement door. He thought nothing of the snowmobile being in my room.

"Dad's gonna bring me to the gas station; then I can get this thing running."

"Do you think it will run?"

"I hope so—yeah, I think it will!" I said excitedly.

Well, my six dollars filled the five-gallon gas can and got me a quart of two-cycle engine oil with some change to spare. Dad, Jimmy and I were outside in the front yard.

"How much oil should I add to the gas?"

"These old machines run kind of rich. I would add the whole quart and shake it well so it mixes in good. Maybe we should have put the oil in the gas can first. It would've been easier to mix," Dad said.

"Yeah, it's kinda heavy," I answered.

"Well, I'm gonna go in the house and fix something to eat." Dad closed the front door behind him.

"When do you think you'll get it running?"

"I'm not sure, pretty soon though! It needs a little more work and I should be set," I told my brother.

With the gas and oil mixed, into the backyard we went. Mom's clothesline was still up with some extra to spare. I cut off about a three-foot piece with my Swiss Army knife.

"What's that for?" Jimmy asked.

"You'll see," I told him while breaking off a piece of a maple branch that had fallen off a tree. Back inside to the smell of the wood stove and the warmth of the basement. I wrapped one end of the clothesline around the piece of branch and tied a knot on the other side. That'll pull the engine over, I thought, as I chucked it on my bed.

"What's left to do?" Jimmy asked.

"Not too much! I should see if it will run before I put it back together," I answered.

Right then, I heard Dad come down the basement stairs. He walked over, "How far are ya?"

"Well, I'd like to start it up before taking it back outside.

"What are you going to use to pull it over?"

"Oh, I got a piece of rope with a handle on it."

"Alright, grab the gas can and we'll put enough in to see if it runs or not." After putting in about a half a tank full, Dad stuffed a rag in for a makeshift gas cap. "Where is that rope?" he asked.

"Here it is." I handed it to him. He wrapped it around the flywheel, putting the knotted end in a notch so it wouldn't slip and pulled it over. Nothing! He tried again. Still nothing! Dad went over to the workbench and came back with a can of starting fluid.

"We'll spray a little of this in and see what happens." Again he pulled the flywheel over. Still nothing! It's got to run—not all this work for nothing I thought! He wrapped the rope.

"Well, do you think she's gonna run?

"I hope so!" He pulled it over. It fired! It was flooded out and filled the basement with white smoke as it barely sputtered to life. Since the throttle cable wasn't hooked up, he revved the engine, moving the butterfly valve by hand. The track spun. It seemed to work great. Our basement was full of the oily gasoline smelling smoke. We let it run a few minutes until it ran smooth then shut it off. All of a sudden I heard the top door open.

"Dear, what are you doing? The whole house smells like gasoline!" Mom shouted.

"Let's open some windows down here and the door so we can air it out."

"That was cool," Jimmy said.

"Well, finish putting it together so you can bring it outside. I'm sure gonna hear it when I go upstairs," Dad said.

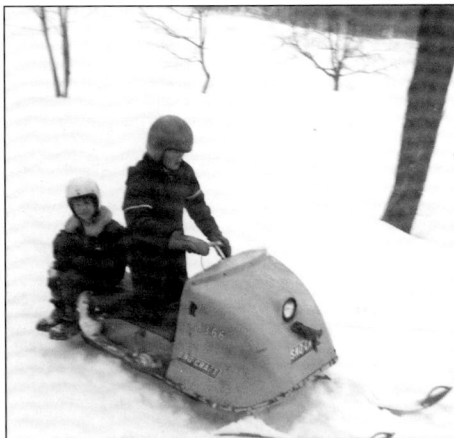

Jeff and his brother Jimmy on the $25 snowmobile.

TEN

In the front yard of the old farmhouse lay huge timbers twenty feet long and about two feet square. I wonder what Irvin's up to now, I thought while looking at the freshly delivered pile. My snowmobile adventures through the backyard and woods were more troublesome than fun. The machine wouldn't turn very well because there was no wear rods on the skis, sometimes leaving me off the trail in places where the snow was deep and powdery. On a few occasions I yelled out every cuss word I could think of and even made up some of my own while digging the sled out and getting back on track. It seemed that every corner we went around, it would get stuck so I had my brother ride on the back with a shovel. The throttle cable would keep me from going wide open because of how it was connected. It fouled out spark plugs a few times a day and was just a wreck. Oh well, live and learn. I'm thankful that I didn't spend any more than what I did.

The winter was getting long and cold—I needed a break. What better time to see my old friend. Right then from around the corner of the house, came Irvin all bundled up, carrying a pitchfork and basket.

"Hey Jeff, how ya doing?"

"Good, haven't seen you in a while, just wondering what's going on?"

"Well, I was just about to go get a few parsnips and turnips from the garden. A lady friend dropped off a ham bone and cornbread, so now I'm gonna make some boiled dinner."

"Yeah, sounds good. Ma makes that once in a while on these cold days." How's he going to dig up anything? The ground is frozen, but knowing him, he had his ways so I didn't question it. When we got to the snow covered garden, Irvin turned over some straw with the pitchfork.

"See, Jeff, this keeps the soil from freezing. I'll be able to get these out of the ground with no problem." I watched as he dug up a dozen of each.

"Why so many?" I asked.

"I'll give some to the neighbors. It's good to help people out."

"Yeah, you always have somebody over helping you out, too."

"This place is a big operation. I got so many projects going on, I can use all the help I can get. How's things at home?"

"Pretty good."

"What brings you here today?"

"I was just wondering how you've been."

"Do your parents know you're here?"

"Yep."

"Good. I got a pile of wood delivered yesterday. Maybe you can give me a hand with it."

"Those are huge pieces of wood. Where did they come from?"

"They're beams off an old warehouse that was torn down. The wrecking crew needed to get rid of them, so I took em."

"What are you gonna do with them?"

"I'll show you when we get back to the house."

While Irvin knelt down and began filling the basket with parsnips, I looked at the many rows of white bee boxes on the crusted snow. In front of them lay hundreds of dead honeybees.

"I need to get a queen bee and start a new colony this spring," Irvin said while standing up. "Well, let's get going."

"Alright," I answered. Irvin's hands were full, carrying the basket, so I grabbed the pitchfork and back to the house we went.

Irvin set the basket down in the entryway, next to the potatoes and squash.

"You still have them out here?" I asked.

"Yep, potatoes and squash will keep a while as long as they are cool and dry."

We went back outside. I closed the storm door behind me. Leaning against the side of the house was a two-man crosscut saw. Irvin grabbed it. As we headed towards the stack of timbers, a big dog ran past and down the road. "He's back! I'm gonna shoot that thing!" Irvin shouted."

Why? What's wrong?" I asked.

"I have a couple of geese down by the barn. That dog got into them and pulled half of their feathers out."

"Looks like he's gone now. If he comes back, I'll shoot him for ya," I said.

The timbers were laid out in a way that they were easy to sort out. On one of them, I noticed an oil can and sawdust where a section had been cut. "You ready?" Irvin asked while setting the long blade on top of a beam.

"Yes, I am."

"Alright. When I pull the saw towards me, don't push it forward. Let the saw do the work. Then once the blade is all the way on my side, you pull."

"Got it," I answered.

We started sawing the thick piece of wood. When about half way, the crosscut was getting harder to pull. "It's starting to bind," Irvin said. Taking the oil can, he squirted some onto both sides of the blade. After that the saw sliced the other half like a knife through butter. "Wood heats the house good, but coal's even better. It burns a long time with a steady heat. I would like to get a truckload full but no one is selling it these days," said Irvin.

With one good sized chunk of timber cut, we started on another. "We'll cut one more piece. These will be big enough to heat the house for the night. I won't split them so they'll burn 'til morning." A strong gust of wind blew past. I felt its cold chill as it put a dusting of crystal-like snow on my face. The tall pines around the house swayed as the old brick chimney left a swirl of white smoke. The smell of wood smoke, along with the sharp winter air stung my nostrils and made my eyes water. Then with one last pull of the saw's handle, its sharp blade made its way through the timber. "That should do it!" Irvin shouted, while leaning the crosscut against the snow covered stack of wood.

"Well, let's get these inside and we'll take a break," said Irvin. With that, each of us grabbed a piece and headed towards the house. Along the way, I saw the old tractor now with tire chains and a little snow left in its bucket.

"Yea, I plowed a few driveways out this morning—just being neighborly and helping out, ya know. That left tire has a leak in it. I've got too much work going on to fix it any time soon. I'll fill it with air as need be."

Reaching the doorway, we heard the geese down below honking and flapping their wings about. "He's down there again! I had a feeling that dog would be back." Right then both of us dropped the wood next to the turnip basket, Irvin reached in the corner where a winter coat hung, lifted it and grabbed his .22 rifle from underneath, "Let's get 'em!"

Running down the driveway and into the backyard, we saw the geese outside their shed. They were plucked nearly bald, just like a turkey ready for the oven. They were frantic, running in all directions—there was much commotion. All of a sudden, from around the corner of the shed, snarling and showing its teeth was the big red dog! Irvin reached into his pocket and got a bullet, loaded the rifle then handed it to me. The wild dog ran towards an open field and stopped. I took aim and fired! The dog yelped then took off.

"Aaaahhh, ya missed 'em."

"I'm sure I got him, let's go see."

Over to the field we walked. There was no sign of the dog anywhere and no hole in the snow where the bullet should've left a hole. So, whether I hit him or not remained a mystery.

It was about suppertime when I started my walk home. I passed the stonewall, where the old man had sat on that nice fall day. "I wonder where he is and if he's okay," I thought. Right then the wind picked up snow and drifted it across the bank, leaving a white haze around a streetlight above. I pushed my hands deeper into the coat pockets, trying to stay warm. "Hmm, I wonder what Mom's cookin' tonight. A hot meal would sure be good about now."

ELEVEN

Reaching the driveway, I noticed the station wagon wasn't there. This usually meant the whole family would be gone. Not much snow fell throughout the day, but the driveway was scraped clean. I walked up the back porch and inside the kitchen. It was dark except for the light coming from the open door that led to the basement. The warmth of our home welcomed me from the bitter cold outside. I took off my jacket, laying it across the kitchen table. Right then, my brother popped through the door with his new pet rat, Ben, in his hands. "Where have you been?" He asked.

"Oh, I just stopped by Uncle Irvin's."

"What for?"

"Well, I hadn't talked to him for a while so I just wanted to see what he was up to. What's going on around here?" I asked Jimmy.

"Not much. Everyone got together at Trotta's." They were our great aunts.

Jimmy pulled out a chair and sat at the kitchen table. Ben crawled across his shoulder scratching Jimmy's bare neck. "Ahhh!" Jimmy shrieked. I sat down, too, on the other side while my brother put Ben on the table's polished surface.

I opened the *Duluth Herald* and looked through the want ads. It was always fun to see what was for sale or what types of jobs were available in the area. After a few minutes Jimmy was laughing. I put down the newspaper and looked. Ben's feet were kicking from behind. He couldn't get a grip on the slippery tabletop. I started laughing too. We took turns pushing Ben back and forth, sliding him towards each other. After a couple of minutes or so, he was tired and breathing rapidly from trying to run. "Alright, that's enough, Ben," Jim said while placing him back upon his shoulder.

I got up to get a drink of water. Taking the glass from the cupboard and filling it, I noticed the large octagon shaped jar full of pipe tobacco Dad brought home a while ago. Mom just wanted the nice looking jar and hadn't emptied it yet. After drinking, I set the glass down. I had an idea, and in no time, we were downstairs at the old work bench. I grabbed the red handled bucksaw Dad kept hanging on the wall and went outside. All I had on was my red and black checkered flannel shirt. In the backyard, next to the clothesline, lay a couple of dead maple branches. They were about an inch and a half in diameter. "What are you doing?" Jimmy asked, while standing in the doorway.

"You'll see." Anxiously, I cut off a piece about a foot long. Chilled from the cold winter air, I ran back inside, closing the door behind me. In a hurry, I cut a two inch piece and clamped it in the vice. Opening the work bench drawer, I took out a hand power drill. I looked on the shelf above for the largest drill bit. "I still have no idea what you're doing," Jimmy said.

"Just watch." With the sawed end of the branch facing upwards, I drilled into it about a good inch deep, then grabbed a smaller bit, drilling through the side. Looking down, I could see I was through. "Perfect!"

On the bottom of the workbench there were plumbing supplies. Quickly, I sorted through the different size pieces of pipe and tubing until I found what I thought would do the trick. There was a length of copper tubing about three feet long and around the size of a pencil in diameter. I cut a six inch piece off with a hacksaw and grabbed the drilled out maple branch from the vice then pushed and twisted the copper into the smaller hole. "Well, whattya think of this?" I asked Jimmy.

"Looks like a pipe for smoking."

"You're right – that's what it is."

"I got a feeling you're gonna try that tobacco we found in the cupboard, aren't you?"

"Yep."

"Will ya help me make a pipe, too?"

"Yea, then we'll have a fire and roast a few hotdogs!" I said with excitement.

"Cool! I'll just put Ben back in his cage," Jimmy answered.

Putting our parkas on, we ran upstairs into the kitchen. Mom, Dad, and our sisters were still gone. With hot dogs, homemade pipes, and a little tobacco from the jar in our pockets, we stepped out into the deep freeze. By now the gusty winds had stopped and the full moon lit up the white winter wonderland with its brightness.

Up a small hill, on the other side of the frozen cedar swamp was a special place in the woods where my brother and I would go to have campfires and just hang out. It's a flat open space nestled under huge white pines. In its center was half of a 55 gallon steel oil drum. Before I knew it, we were there gathering deadfall in the almost daylight surroundings. Soon we had a good sized pile of wood and a fire going so hot inside the drum its steel was glowing red.

It was time to sit down and enjoy our winter campsite. A few feet away from the barrel lay a large log we used for a bench. Brushing the snow off, we both sat down. I took my gloves off and leaned forward with open hands to feel the fire's toasty warmth.

Jimmy took the pipe from his jacket. "Should we test them?" he asked.

"I was just thinking the same thing," I said, while taking mine from my pocket.

"Where's the tobacco?"

"I got it," as I began packing the pipe. Jimmy watched. The pine tree had a long dead branch. I broke it off, sticking the smallest end into the hot coals. I got it burning almost instantly. Holding it over the pipe, I took several puffs.

"Hey, this works great," I told Jimmy. Jimmy's was already packed and ready to light. "Here you go," I said, holding the lighted stick over his pipe.

"What do I do?"

"Just do like I did and you'll get it goin'."

The snow around the hot steel drum was melting, leaving a two foot space around its base. The little bit of snow that stuck to our jeans melted, making steam roll off the cuffs of our pants and boot laces.

"My pipe keeps goin' out," Jimmy said, while trying to relight it.

"Maybe you packed the tobacco too hard. Loosen it up and try again."

I took a few more puffs of my pipe, thinking about how it must have been when a trapper went to the trading post to cash in his furs. Then I stood up and put more wood on the fire in a teepee like fashion. "We're gonna have a really good fire in a few minutes."

"Yea, then we should cook them hotdogs," Jimmy said, while taking a few more puffs from his pipe.

"Is that burning better?" I asked.

"Seems to be."

"Well let's get some sticks for roasting."

Looking around we found a couple of long spindly branches. I didn't have my knife so we just broke them off. They were still green, not dried out like the one we used for lighting our pipe—perfect for cooking hotdogs. They wouldn't burn in half, leaving the meal plopped into the fire.

Back at the campfire, we sat down. I was feeling kind of queasy and light headed. Hanging the pipe in a nearby tree branch so it wouldn't get lost in the snow, I put a hotdog on one of the green sticks. My brother must have felt the same way and hung his pipe too. Both of us were quiet while roasting the dogs. With all the wood I put on the fire, it was really going. There was a cedar tree close to the flames. Its branches swayed from the heat rising. A bunch of snow fell off, just missing the fire.

"Nothing like a hotdog over a fire, with the surface bubbly black and slightly crunchy," I remarked. The juicy dog was almost done. A few drops fell into the hot cinders, sizzling. It smelled delicious. Done enough for me, I thought, letting the dog cool off wouldn't take long. I'm sure the temperature was easily 10 below, maybe more. With everything so cold and frozen, I often wondered where all the small creatures went in the depths of winter.

"Mmmm, man, these hotdogs are good! I let mine get pretty dark too."

I tested the dog, "Yup."

Suddenly we heard footsteps crunching in the snow and saw a figure coming up the hill towards us. "Hey what are you guys up too? I saw the fire from your backyard and thought I'd come down." It was our friend, Dennis. My brother and I finished our hotdogs and threw the sticks in the fire.

"Man! It's cold out!" Dennis remarked and warmed up by the fire. "What are you guys doin' out here?"

"Just thought we'd cook some hotdogs." Jimmy answered.

Right then Dennis spit in the fire and put a few pieces of wood in. "Yeah, I've been working on my snowmobile."

"What's wrong with it?" Jimmy asked.

"I hit the side of a tree and the left ski is bent inward."

"Must be out of alignment," I said.

"Yeah, it's way off," he answered, while walking towards the log to sit down. "Cool! Who's pipe is this?" Dennis asked, while grabbing it from the tree and putting it in his mouth. His eyes got huge. Out of the corner of his mouth he tried shouting.

"What's wrong?" I asked

"I can't get this thing out of my mouth! What am I gonna do?" The copper tubing had gotten so cold in the minus zero weather that it stuck onto his lips and tongue. In a panic, he yanked the pipe from his mouth. We stared as he let out a streak of cuss words. His lips were bleeding. It looked like some skin stuck to the copper.

"Man that sucked bad!" Dennis said. "My tongue is bleeding, too!"

"Let me take a look," I told him.

He stuck his tongue out. Sure enough, it was bleeding a little bit.

"How bad is it?" he asked.

"Pretty bad. Looks like all your taste buds got ripped off and you'll never taste again."

"NO WAY!" he shouted.

"I'm just kidding. Would you relax? Put some snow on your mouth—it'll be okay."

"I'm just gonna go home," said Dennis, "Besides, I gotta pee."

"Me too," Jimmy replied and, like all guys I'm sure have done, we relieved ourselves at the same time, trying to put the fire out. The fire wasn't completely extinguished so we kicked snow on it and left the campsite.

TWELVE

I peered out my bedroom window, it's edges now had a light layer of ice forming and was fogged over. I could hardly see a thing. Taking my shirtsleeve, I wiped a clear spot then looked out again. The thermometer my parents hung on a big maple tree read fifteen above zero, and it was snowing lightly outside. "Hmmm, what should I do today?" While thinking it over, I walked over to my desk. On top was a good-sized cooler with its lid gone.

The week before, Jimmy and I walked up to a local bait shop. We were curious to see if they carried sling shots.

"How can I help you boys today?" The man behind the cash register asked.

"We were wondering if you sold sling shots up here?"

"Yes, we sure do, they are right there on the top shelf towards the back."

"Okay, we'll have a look," I replied.

When my brother and I reached the back of the bait shop we noticed several bait tanks containing chubs, shiners, crappie minnows and on the end, a sign, which read 'Light Pike.' We looked in the cold bubbly water and saw two salamanders, greenish with yellow spots.

"Yeah, those are leopard salamanders. They just happened to be mixed in with the delivery," the owner said, while taking a sip of coffee.

"Cool. Are they for sale?"

"They could be."

"How much?"

"I'll let ya have both of them for a dollar."

"What do you think?" I asked my brother.

"Yea, let's get 'em – that would be cool," he answered back.

"What do they eat?"

"Worms."

"Okay, I'll take a dozen night crawlers too."

"What will you do with them?"

"I think they'll be cool to have at home."

"Yea, I think you'll enjoy them. I've sold several in the past week for aquariums."

As the owner was getting the salamanders ready, we looked at the sling shots. There were several kinds, one had a wood handle in the usual "Y" shape. I picked it up grabbed the leather pouch and pulled back. It went too easy. This wouldn't shoot far, I thought. Jimmy opened a box, there was one similar to this, only with a plastic handle. Neither of these would do. I knew what I came for. I wanted a wrist rocket, one of the most powerful sling shots made. I read about this sling shot in *Outdoor Life* magazine. It would be good for hunting small game and target practice.

Hmmm….there's got to be one in here somewhere. Right when I was going to ask for help, I spotted it. There was only one left sitting under the other boxes. I opened the box and took it out—just what I wanted, the same one as advertised in the magazine.

"Are you sure there's not another one?" My brother asked, while moving the other boxes of sling shots around.

"Looks like this is the only one," I answered.

Right then the owner bagged up the salamanders, "Did you find what you're looking for?" he asked, while tightening the rubber band around the top of the water filled bag.

"Yes we did, but there's only one left. Do you have anymore in stock?"

"No, but if you're not in a hurry I have something similar you might be interested in." He walked into the back room and in a couple of minutes came back. "This is a fold up version wrist rocket. It's kind of neat. You can fit it right in your jacket pocket. I don't use it much anymore, and I can see both of you want one. Tell you what—I'll give you a reasonable price. How does three dollars sound?" he asked my brother.

"I guess so. What do you think, Jeff?"

"I think it's a good deal. Get it and we'll both have one."

"Okay."

With that we put our hard earned snow shoveling money on the counter. "Well, I'm sure you'll have fun. Have a good day now."

"Thanks a lot! We will. "Then we took off out the door. "Man, you got a good deal! My wrist rocket was five bucks. I think the one you got is better and you only paid three." Both of us were happy and started the five mile long walk home.

Well, we brought the salamanders home and here they are, in the cooler with about six inches of water and a good sized stone in the center for them to crawl on. Deciding they must be hungry I broke a night crawler into bite sized pieces. That should do it. I was excited to watch them eat. Both of them gulped down a couple pieces eagerly then found their way to the corners of the tank.

I was content watching them, wondering what lake they came from. Then fishing came to mind. Enough of the salamanders. I grabbed my tackle box from the closet, set it on the desk next to the cooler and looked inside. It was a mess! I sat on my bed and took everything from the box. Besides all the fishing tackle, there were a couple dried up leaves, chewing gum wrappers, and even a couple dehydrated minnows stuck to the bottom, not to mention a little dirt and sand. With all the contents now on my bed, I took the empty tackle box over to the laundry sink and rinsed it out. After drying it, I sat down. Taking my time, I began putting things back. Spoons, rappalas, crank baits went in the two fold out compartments. Bobbers, fishhooks, sinkers, a fillet knife, spare fishing line went on the bottom. As I organized it, I daydreamed about good fishing times I had and those I will have when spring gets here.

Dad was up to something. I got up; set the tackle box on the floor. Walking towards the workshop, I could see he was going through tins of gunpowder, empty shotgun shells, primers and wads.

"Are you gonna reload some 12 gauge?" I asked.

"Not today, just straightening things out around here."

"Can I load up a box of 20 gauge?"

"I suppose. I was going through my reloading supplies and found these three bags. They're almost empty but we will use what's left. I've got 7 1/2, 6, and number 4 shot."

As Dad held one of the bags open, I emptied the other two into it, mixing all 3 shot sizes together. I took the red cover off the re-loader and Dad filled it. "This should be a good game load," he said, "just clean things up when you're done."

Pulling a stool next to the workbench, I sat down in front of the shot shell reloader. Hmmm, primers, wads, a couple dozen empty shot shells—I was all set to reload. I started reloading the empty shells while Dad put deer hunting gear in order.

It was before noon on one of those cold winter days when everyone was just sitting around the house. Mom was in the kitchen mixing batter for her new waffle iron. Jimmy was in his room playing with his pet rat. Dad went back upstairs and my sisters were going to watch Mom make waffles. Again the old cast iron wood stove was doing its duty and kept the house toasty warm. It was a good thing I brought in plenty of firewood weeks earlier.

Reloading shotgun shells was enjoyable and relaxing to me. I would daydream about the hunt as I loaded each shell, one by one. How many partridge or rabbits would I see, or if it was big game season, would I get that big buck? I could hunt most wild game in this neck of the woods with a shotgun. That's what I liked about my Savage 20-guage pump action that Dad had given me. I could use shot shells on small game and slugs for deer. Come to think of it, if I could only own one gun, it would have to be a shotgun.

As I daydreamed on with half of the shells reloaded, I remembered not too long ago, Mom and Dad went out for the evening, leaving Jackie to watch over my younger sisters, Annette, Sherry, Kristie and my brother Jimmy. The evening was going well, everyone was in the living room eating hot, buttered popcorn Jackie had just made and watching TV. It wasn't too long when Jackie went into the kitchen for something to drink. Upon doing so, she noticed what at first appeared to be a large black dog sitting out on the back porch. She thought nothing of it and got a bottle of pop from the fridge. It was then, as she turned toward the cupboard to get a glass, there stood the biggest black bear ever, standing on its hind legs. She ran into the living room, "Oh my Gosh! Oh my Gosh! There's a huge bear on the back porch you guys! I've never seen one that big before! I'm gonna call the game warden!"

Quite shocked and scared, they waited hoping the big bear would stay away. About twenty minutes later the Game Warden pulled into the driveway. Jackie opened the door.

"So ya have a bear bigger than you've ever seen coming up the porch?"

"Yea, he was just here."

"Okay, I'll have a look around." Everyone looked out the dining room window as the game warden took his flashlight and searched the backyard. About ten minutes later, Jackie welcomed him into the kitchen. "Well, I didn't see any sign back there."

"Can I make you a cup of coffee?" Jackie asked.

"That would be nice. It's rather chilly out tonight. So, you kids saw the bear, too?"

"Yea—he's huge!"

"Okay. Well, I'll stay awhile just to be on the safe side." Jackie poured a cup of fresh hot coffee. "Thank you. Yea, our office has been getting a lot of calls. Seems there's a problem with bears everywhere." He no sooner said that when Jackie shouted, "There he is!"

Looking out onto the back porch, "I'll be darned!" said the game warden. The bear took towards the backyard. "I'll be back in a minute." He went to his car and returned with a 12-guage. The bear had climbed a big maple tree down near the tin shed. Seeing that the bear was so large from feeding through the neighborhood and that he could be a danger, the officer shot and killed it.

About then, Mom and Dad pulled into the driveway. My friend Ed and I crossed the street, coming from his house. We were both carrying Daisy bb guns from a day of shooting cans and bottles. My sisters and brother were outside. Uncle Ed, who lived next door, came over too see what was going on. Dad called his friend Wally down. Someone brought a snowmobile trailer by and all the guys loaded the bear onto it. As the bear lay there and everyone was talking about the evening's event, my brother and I felt a front leg on the bear. What a strong animal it must have been, we both thought.

Mmmmmm, the smell of breakfast was in the air, and the ammunition reloaded for another day. I met Jimmy at the basement stairs, "Let's eat, I'm starving!"

"Me too," he said, "Can't wait to taste those homemade waffles!"

THIRTEEN ❧

Just outside the basement door, it had been snowing since early morning. The kind of snow that was fluffy but looked to be just a bit on the sticky side. I knelt down, tightening each leather strap on my snowshoes. The big flakes fell gently, leaving a frosty coating on all the tree branches. I grabbed a handful. The snow was just right as I packed a perfect hard snowball. Standing up, I looked around. The smell of winter and fresh snow was crisp in the air. According to the big round thermometer, it warmed up a little outside. Right then, I whipped the snowball hard. The glass covering shattered. I didn't even think about how much work it must have been for my parents to put that up. Well, it should still work, I thought.

Earlier at the breakfast table, I broke the bacon in small pieces, placing them along with a fried egg on top of the waffles, then smothering the works in maple syrup. This was one of my favorites.

Still plenty full from breakfast, I needed to get away. It was fairly nice out, but up north, 'Old Man Winter' could go from good to downright freezing. Knowing this I dressed prepared. Wearing a parka, which would keep me warm in most cold weather, choppers for my hands, winter pacs for my feet, and a cap on my head. Since I planned on being a ways from home, matches for fire, and a couple hot dogs. Leaning next to the basement was my bow, I grabbed it along with three arrows. I was set for a day in the woods.

I stepped forward onto the soft new blanket of snow. Each snowshoe sank a few inches but still, they kept me from sinking almost knee-deep into the powdery stuff. The going was fairly easy. As I looked onto the field below, I knew just where I was going to go. I would cut through our woods and follow a trail I knew very well, which led to the countryside.

Standing under the old oak tree, I looked up. It had shed its colorful autumn leaves. Only a few dried brown ones clung to its snow covered branches—quite a change from only a few months ago. Ahead of me where tall grass grew their brown blades now poked through the snow's powdery surface, along with the little bulbs of many goldenrods. Right then, I thought of something I had learned in a nature class. Inside each bulb hibernates a wax worm. If you should need bait for ice fishing, they work well for blue gills and panfish. All you do is cut the bulb in half with your knife and get the little grub out. A couple of dozen of these and you're set. I continued onward. This time instead of heading towards the cedar swamp, I took a left which led me to another a field. Around its borders grew many sumacs with their red fuzzy berries still hanging on. Sometimes I would pick off a few and suck on them. They were tangy. After the tartness was gone, I spit out the seeds. I heard they contain Vitamin C and are a good source of energy if you should get lost.

Ahead the trail sloped downward leading to a stretch of tall maples and poplar trees. Earlier that spring on a bright sunny day when everything was in bloom and the grass was knee deep I stirred up a covey of partridge. One by one, six of them burst from the green cover. The loud fluttering and flapping sound of their wings is enough to make your heart stop on a quiet day. Today the sky was filled with gray clouds, the kind that just hung there and never seemed to move. About halfway through the path of tall trees there was a hill on the left side. Part way up I noticed a good sized hole dug under the rooted area of a large tree. There were many small paw prints on the snow's surface leading in and out. I wondered what could be living in there. I've seen many skunks, porcupines and raccoons—could it be one of them? Near the end of the tall wooded area was a small creek. As I looked down I saw the water trickle under its icy surface and flow into the swamp below. I crossed. The trail took a sharp left leading up to a very steep hill. It started out gradual at first. As it sloped steeper, I gripped the bow tightly and began pointing the front tips of each snowshoe outward. This way, I had good traction and could go straight up where the hill was steeper yet. Come to think of it, imagine a duck walking up hill—that's what it must look like. Finally, reaching the top, my reward was a breathtaking view! The peak overlooked the whole woods and in the giant meadow below leaped four doe and the huge buck I saw earlier that fall while I was rabbit hunting.

As I overlooked the woods below, a thought crossed my mind. Often times during the summer, even on the hottest, clearest day, up here or through Mom's kitchen window, you could watch an eerie dense layer of fog suddenly roll over the tree line, swooping down and blanketing the swamp with its ghostliness. Why was this? Because just a few miles away sits one of the biggest, coldest, and deepest lakes in the world, Lake Superior. I don't know the reasons that cause this phenomenon, but living next to this great body of water is an experience in itself. Great ships from all over the world arrive through the canal and under one of the most unique bridges, the Duluth Aerial Lift Bridge. It crosses the canal so vehicles can drive from downtown Duluth to Park Point, then lifts as the captain from the ship blows its horn three times. Once in the harbor, the bridge lowers again, and the ships dock, either full of grain or empty so they can export iron ore. Fishermen also make a living on the big lake either as guides for fishing trips, or commercially bringing in lake trout, salmon, and white fish to the local markets.

To me, whenever things get hectic or were moving too fast in the world, a good long walk through the woods like today seemed to take it all away. I would forget about the stresses of school and other things like having enough money. None of that mattered right now. It's out here I find the peace and beauty only nature can bring to the soul. A gift from God, free for the taking.

Big fluffy snowflakes gently fell from the grey clouds above. I looked up, ahead of me were oak and more tall maple trees. In many of them were clumps of brown dead leaves where squirrels nested. I took another step forward, a steady but gentle breeze swept by, rustling the small but well built shelters. I thought for sure something would jump, but it wasn't to be. Just off to my left, about ten feet up in a small oak tree, were a few grayish weathered boards, the remains of a deer stand from years past. I wondered…did the hunter who sat there see such a big buck as I did today?

There were many deer that crossed this pasture like area. The trail was heavy with hoof prints, some bigger and deeper than others. I followed. It was well traveled, which made the going on snowshoes a little easier. In some parts of the field I could see where they bed down for the night, leaving their packed nestled outlines on the grass and snow. Reaching the other side, I noticed swamp where the herd ran through, splashing dark brown muddy water on the fresh white covering.

Leaving the muddied area behind and still following the deer trail, I entered an apple orchard. The trees had been there many years producing fruit. Work-hands from the Great Depression labored in the back 100 acres, clearing and plowing the land. Great sized gardens were planted and dairy cattle roamed the green grassy pastures, producing milk in abundance. Just ahead on the other side of the orchard was a huge barn that once sheltered the cattle—it stood the test of time. I'm sure this old place hasn't changed much, I thought, looking up at the rusted weather vane creaking in the wind.

I knew about how the land used to be because Irvin would bring it up from time to time, either at his place or ours, especially at the dining room table while having coffee. Being a dairy farmer himself he would tell stories about the Depression my family and I always enjoyed. How if you lived on a farm, there was always food on the table, either from the vegetables in the garden, meat from pigs, chickens, and cows or fresh milk from the Dairy. So, on a farm you'd know where your next meal was coming from and you wouldn't go hungry like so many others did during the Depression.

As I stood next to the big old barn, I looked back at the apple orchard, wondering how it must have been years ago. Many times while exploring this part of the woods, Jimmy, my sisters, and I would find old plates, spoons, forks, a couple coffee pots, not to mention many whiskey and wine bottles. Aunt Kate, Mom's sister, would tell us about how hobos and drifters camped out there in hopes of finding work on the big farm, whether it be for a meal or a little money to get a bottle of booze they would share at the campsite. Even after the Depression it sounded like times were tough. Mom, Aunt Kate, and my four uncles, Jerry, Tommy, Stewart and Louie grew up in the same house we were living. They cut many trees down by hand to heat the place. Meat was often times too expensive to buy, so when they were tired of eating canned beans, the guys would hunt. There was plenty of wild game out there—deer, geese, ducks, rabbits, partridge—it didn't matter. It was all good meat for the pot and those were tough times to be choosey. One summer, Uncle Jerry caught a 50 pound snapping turtle he brought home to eat, and in the fall—a big bull moose he hunted with his 30-06 rifle.

If the woods could only talk, what tales they would tell!

The bindings on my snowshoes had loosened from the walk.

Setting the bow and three arrows down onto the snow, I took the leather choppers off. My hands were quite warm and steamed slightly in the crisp air; I tightened each strap. This is where I wanted to be. Just behind the barn stood many pine trees, different in size and all covered in white—a good spot to hunt, I thought, while grabbing my bow and taking each step quietly.

It was dead silent out when suddenly, from a tall pine, a big white owl swooped down gracefully, catching something in the field below, then disappeared quickly like a thief in the night. It was quite a sight! If it was a mouse, I'm sure the critter never knew what happened. I hunted this place for a while, looking for partridge. In the winter time, these game birds like to stay put so some times you can almost sneak right up on them. That's what I was hoping for as I looked under the evergreens where they like to hide, but there was none to be found, just droppings and their chicken-like foot prints.

With no luck here, I found another deer trail and cut through. It led to a good sized garden which people from the community still planted. Rows of dried corn stalks stood upright, half buried in the snow. Sometimes pheasants would stick around here even during winter. I decided to walk through—no pheasants here. I knew the chances of getting one with a bow were slim at best, but maybe I could catch one off guard and get 'em. I heard they were good eating, I'd like to find that out for myself.

Earlier that fall, Mom said there wouldn't be any homemade pickles to eat because her cucumber patch died off. Jimmy and Jackie felt bad, so one afternoon they brought a wagon of Jimmy's here and returned home with plenty of cucumbers for Mom to pickle.

Soon it would be dark, but there was still enough time to cut through the woods to Irvin's—I did. Hunting all sides and outer edges of the huge garden, there weren't even any rabbit tracks; the snow that had fallen earlier covered them for sure. By now I found myself on the far bottom side of Irvin's land. Dusk had set in. When I did reach the farmhouse, it was pitch black out except for the northern lights with their prism-like colors streaking across sky. I walked by looking in the window, Irvin was at the table eating dinner by the glow of an old-fashioned oil lamp. Too tired to stop in and say hi, I went home, got my winter clothes off and made a hot cup of tea.

I didn't bag any game—that's how it goes sometimes; just being out there made my day.

FOURTEEN 🐾

This time of year winter really sets in and seems like it will never end, but as the sun sets later in the evening, you'd keep reminding yourself spring was just around the corner and would be here before you knew it. I remember Mom told me Uncle Art said, "You shouldn't wish winter away too soon because summer goes by so fast and is gone in no time at all." No words spoken in this part of the country could be truer.

Dennis' lip healed up just fine from the pipe incident. I'd sold the 'thorn in my side' snowmobile to a neighbor. Maybe he would have some luck fixing it up. I even took a walk all the way over to the power line where Dad, John, and I deer hunted that fall and got a few rabbits with my 20-guage. Those shells I reloaded with Dad's mixed shot idea sure came in handy. Wanting to try something different, I ended up deboning two of the rabbits and ground the meat in a blender. When that was done, I added some sage, Italian seasoning, salt, black pepper, a little red pepper, mixed it together well and made patties. They smelled delicious, sizzling in the frying pan. Mom took the other rabbit, stuffed it with dressing, a recipe she used on Thanksgiving, wrapped bacon around the whole works and baked it. Both of our ideas turned out good. My mom and dad tried a little, but I was the only one that really ate the wild game. The rest of the family didn't care to.

And right now, I was in my bedroom, sitting in front of the desk, waxing the slightly frayed string on my bow. All three rabbit hides were stretched and tacked on a piece of plywood next to the wood pile. I thought when they're done drying they might look nice on the wall. Right then Jimmy walked in with a sad look on his face and Ben in his hands. It was just before noon.

"Ben's dead."

"What happened?"

"I don't know. I found him on the floor next to my bed."

"Maybe he fell and got hurt."

"What am I going to do? It's cold out and the ground is frozen solid. I won't be able to bury him."

"Hmmmm, I've got an idea. Hold on a second…be right back." I went into the canning room. I felt bad Ben died. I looked around and found something. On a shelf was an empty coffee can, I grabbed it and showed it to my brother.

"What are you gonna do with that?" he asked.

"We'll put Ben in here and freeze him. Then when summer gets here, we'll make a grave for him."

"Okay, but we should make him comfortable—not just put him in a steel can," Jimmy pleaded.

"I know we'll find something." I felt sorry for my brother. On the side of my pillow was a tear, I reached in pulling out some cotton-like material. "This will work." I lined the inside of the can and let Jimmy put Ben inside. "He'll be comfortable 'til summer."

Both of us walked over to the chest freezer. I opened it while Jimmy found a good spot and placed Ben on a level package of frozen corn. We closed the freezer.

"Are you okay?" I asked.

"I'll miss Ben. His cage will be empty now," Jimmy said, walking towards his room. I followed. My brother stared into the empty cage.

"You'll find something to put in there," I assured him.

I heard the door open at the top of the stairs. "I think he's down in his room," said Mom.

"Okay." I recognized the voice. It was my friend Ed. Down the stairs he came.

"What's up?" he asked.

"Not too much."

"What's in the cooler?"

"A couple salamanders Jimmy and I got at the bait shop."

"Cool. Let me see. What do they eat?" Ed asked while looking at them.

"Worms."

"Do you have any? I want to see them eat."

"I do, but they already ate. I don't think they're hungry."

"Let's just see."

"Okay," I replied hesitantly. After getting the worms from the fridge I walked over to the desk.

"How do you feed them?"

"You gotta break up the worm and then they'll eat the pieces."

"Let's see if they'll eat a whole one," Ed insisted. I took one of the night crawlers from the bait box and ran the worm between my fingers to get the pieces of worm bedding off, then plopped it in the water. One of the salamanders darted forward, grabbing it. With the crawler half way down, the salamander sat there a minute then spit it out.

"Where did you get the hides?" asked Ed.

"I got them a few days ago on the power line."

"Which one?"

"The one up by the Martin Road."

"Oh. What are you gonna do with them?"

"I thought they'd look good on the wall."

"Cool, they will." Right then Jimmy walked in. "What have you been up to?" Ed asked.

"Ben died this morning so we put him in the freezer. Then I can bury him when summer gets here."

"Don't you think that's kinda gross? There's food in the freezer," Ed said with a weird look.

"He's in a coffee can. It's not going to hurt anything. We couldn't just throw him in the garbage," I answered.

"Yea, that would be mean," Jimmy remarked.

"Guess what!" Ed said with excitement. "My dad's taking me to the sporting goods store. We're getting a couple of fish spears."

"I know a spot up on Grand Lake where the water is open."

"Really? What kinda fish are up there?"

"Huge red-horse suckers, northerns, and some bullheads."

"Cool, wanna come up to the lake with us?"

"Yea, when are you going?" I answered, all fired up.

"Well, if we can get the fish spears tonight, we'll go to the lake around noon."

"Alright! I'll be ready. I don't have a fish spear though."

"Don't worry, you can use one of ours. Well, I need to get home. We're having goulash for supper. I'll give you a call later."

"Sounds good."

"Swell," he said.

I could use one of their fish spears, but I've got my own plans.

In the canning room there was a tackle box. I didn't know whose it was but it had been in there for quite some time. Walking over, I opened the door and there it was back in the corner. Let's see if it still had what I was looking for. I opened the green, slightly rusted box. There they were—big fish hooks. I grabbed ten of them and went to my room. Taking a pair of pliers from my tool box, I bent and pulled each hook as straight as I could, then laid them out flat on the hard concrete floor. Taking a hammer, I tapped each one as straight as possible. There was a box of wood used for kindling next to the split firewood. I found a piece about one inch thick, two inches wide and about a foot long. I took my drill and chucked in a tiny drill bit, then made ten tiny holes about one inch apart across the length of wood.

Taking each straightened hook, I pushed them through until the eye was flush with the wood's surface. Now I had ten straightened hooks all in a row and with their barbed tips the speared fish wouldn't fall off. I made a handle from a broom stick. There was one more thing to do. I took a thick piece of copper wire about 15 inches long and pushed its whole length through the eyes and twisted the wire end around the wood with pliers. This was to keep the hooks secure. There, I was all set. It didn't look the greatest but it was mine and I couldn't wait to try it out.

Something smelled delicious—was it chili or tomato soup? I soon found myself in the kitchen to investigate. Mmmm...sloppy Joes and French fries were on the menu. I put two slices of bread on a dinner plate and went over to the stove. Scooping up some of the steaming tomato mixture with a wooden spoon, I smothered both, grabbed a handful of fries and a couple of big home made dill pickles from a mason jar.

I was about to go back to my room when I heard Mom say happily, "Grandma and Grandpa are coming back from Montana to visit."

"When?" I asked.

"Sometime in the spring. Grandpa's got to get some parts for his log lathe."

"That's good," I replied then went back to my room. I sat on the edge of my bed with the plate of food on my lap. I'd set my fish spear on top of the wood pile next to the stretched rabbit hides. There was just something about it—I guess you'd have to like the outdoors like I did to understand. I took a spoonful of the sloppy joes and chewed slowly savoring the flavor. As I looked at the hides, I remembered the time when Ed, his dad, and I went to Ely. We met Ed's grandpa Bernard in the driveway. He had all the camping gear bundled up in green canvas like Duluth packs. We wished him good morning, closing the doors on the new Cherokee Chief Ed's dad had just bought. The heavy scent of pine trees filled the air.

Ed had brought some suckers he snagged in the St. Louis River. Reaching in the cooler, he got them. Soon, all four of us began talking about the canoe trip and which way we should take in to the Boundary Waters. Ed's grandma Helen had just opened the front door on their trailer house which sat amongst pines right above Shagawa Lake. It was one of those nice warm summer mornings. The sun had just peeked up, the lake glistened. A lone cry of a loon echoed in the distance.

Ed ran up the sidewalk. "Are you guys ready for the big trip?" Helen asked. She stepped out onto the porch, wearing a blue dress with a white apron tied around her waist.

"Yes, and I brought some suckers for Grandpa to smoke when we get back." They were both smiling as they greeted each other with a hug.

"Good to see ya!" Helen said while patting his back. "I'll just run these in the house and put them in the freezer. You guys have yourself a good time now!"

After winding through the dirt back roads, we finally arrived at the canoe rental station and signed in. The anticipation of our adventure made the 30 minute jaunt seem longer than it actually was. With gear loaded and two canoes in the water, we were off.

It was a calm day as we paddled across the lake's mirror-like surface, reflecting the blue sky and light fluffy clouds above. Ed's dad and grandpa were in one canoe and Ed and I in another. By now we had the rhythm of each paddle stroke just right, dipping it in without a splash. The canoe seemed to glide easily over the wave's less glassy surface. Then after each stroke, we lifted the paddle from the water and droplets would roll off making little ripples. Each of us did this repeatedly for what seemed to be a good hour. Occasionally, I would see my reflection along with ducks and birds flying as I dipped the paddle.

"You guys getting tired yet?" Ed Sr. asked.

"Nope, I like paddling. I think it's better than using a motor."

He laughed, "We'll see if you feel the same after a couple more hours."

"I'm not tired either," Ed Jr. answered.

"I find it relaxing myself. Time just seems to pass and I don't get hungry or thirsty," Grandpa Bernard remarked.

"How much farther?" Ed Jr. asked.

"Oh, about three more miles and we'll start looking for a campsite," Bernard answered contentedly.

We ventured further and were coming upon a small island close to the shoreline. In between, the water ran over smooth rocks. We got out, stepping in. It was ankle deep. Pulling the canoes up the shallow river-like embankment, we reached the top. Kind of tired now, we all took a 'five' in silence to catch our breath. It was midday. My light flannel shirt was damp from perspiration. Hotter now, I wiped the sweat from my forehead and Ed dipped his head into the lake, while Bernard took off his thick glasses and wiped them with a handkerchief. Ed Sr. looked around and pointed, "Let's head that way. It looks nice over there."

About half way across this body of water came a canoe zipping by with a small outboard clamped to its side. "I bet you guys would like one of them about now," Ed Sr. remarked. I thought it would be a nice break and I'm sure Ed Jr. did too, but still toughing it out, both of us insisted we liked paddling better.

"Hey, over there! I see it. Let's check it out, looks like a cool campsite!" Ed Jr. shouted excitedly. All of us paddled more anxiously and soon found ourselves landing the canoes and setting up camp.

With the four man tent up, a good fire blazing under a steel grate and a big pot of water boiling, Ed Sr. and Bernard were getting ready to cook the evening meal of hamburgers and fried potatoes with onions, while Ed Jr. and I walked the shoreline casting different lures with our fishing poles. Within about twenty minutes I caught a good sized rock bass and a small northern.

The area was beautiful. There was driftwood and brown pine needles washed up on the sandy beach, huge pines as far as the eye could see and the smell of the woods made me feel like I wanted to stay there forever. Well better get back to camp, I thought. I met Ed Jr. back at the canoes. He'd caught a couple of northerns. "Man, supper smells great! Let's get these fish on a stringer and dig in!"

"Yea, I'm starving—can't wait to eat!" I said with excitement. We tied the stringer of fish to the side of a canoe and sat next to the crackling campfire.

"We already ate. Help yourselves," Ed Sr. said. Ed and I dished up and ate, eagerly cleaning our plates. There was nothing left over. Bernard had taken the hot pot of water and set some aside for drinking, the rest was for washing pans, plates, silverware, and ourselves. Daylight was fading into night, mosquitoes hovered over the lake, and I could hear the call of loons. I was tired. It wasn't much longer and we were all in our sleeping bags for the night.

I was in a deep peaceful sleep when something suddenly woke me. Still groggy and not quite awake I thought maybe I just had a dream. In the comfort of the warm sleeping bag I tried to rest again. Then there it was—again it sounded like something was digging through our food. I woke Ed Jr.,

"I think there's a bear out there."

"No way," he said half asleep.

"Really, I think there is."

"There's no bear," Ed Sr. said, "so shut up and go to sleep."

I tried to sleep but just outside the tent something was rummaging through the cooler. Waking up early after finally falling asleep, I found the wrappers from almost all of our food scattered around the campsite. By now, everyone was awake.

Ed Sr. found a package of polish sausage the bear had bitten into. "If we cook them good it shouldn't do anything," he said.

"That bear sure did a number. Looks like we'll have to pack up and go—we're outta food," said Bernard.

"Wait, we can still catch fish to eat and there's the fish we got on the stringer. We can stay another day," Ed Jr. pleaded.

Adding some wood to last night's hot coals, Ed Sr. got a fire going and fried up the polishes. The bear had eaten the fish from the stringer so frying them up for breakfast was out of the question.

We ended up having black coffee and bear-bitten polish sausage for breakfast then packed up. Our adventure into the Boundary Waters was short, but something good came from it. That night, while we were sitting in Ed's grandparent's living room, Helen turned on the radio. We heard that severe thunderstorms and high winds covered the whole area where we were camping. "Thank God for the bear!" Ed shouted, "Or we'd still be out there!" It turned out to be a blessing in disguise. The next couple of days were great. Ed's grandpa showed Ed and I how to sharpen our pocket knives and smoke the suckers Ed Jr. had brought.

Can't wait to spear fish tomorrow, I thought while mopping up sloppy joes with some fries and crunching a homemade pickle. Too tired to bring the plate upstairs, I set it on my desk and went to sleep.

I couldn't wait to try my fish spear. I found myself at the edge of Grand Lake. Ed, his dad, and I had just broken trail. It was around noon just like we'd planned and almost fifty degrees. "The best place is over there," Ed Jr. said. You could hear the excitement in his voice. We started walking the shoreline. Most of the snow had melted on the lake. It looked safe but still we were careful, avoiding any slushy spots. No ice is safe this time of year they say. Cedar trees lined the shore. Some of them grew sideways, almost touching the icy surface. Up ahead was a large area of open water. It ran parallel next to shore. We stepped quietly as not to spook any fish.

Upon reaching the spot we found a pile of dead suckers someone speared and left. We counted sixteen in all. They looked to be around 6 to 10 pounds, just lying with their red fins frozen.

"What a waste," Ed Jr. remarked.

"Yea, why would somebody do that?" I asked.

"Maybe there's too many of them in the lake so some one did this to help the game fish."

"How?" we asked.

"When the good fish spawn the suckers eat their eggs," Ed Sr. told us. With that said we spread out. I went further ahead. Looking in I noticed the water was about three feet deep and the ice was still thick. This looks safe I thought, crouching next to the water's edge and waiting. Suddenly a northern appeared. Its head poked out just under the icy ledge. It sat there for a moment with its gills moving rapidly then came out in plain sight. Well the hooks on my fish spear were no match for the snake-like fish and it darted back under the ice as suddenly as it appeared. Ed Jr. and his dad and I found a shallow muddy pool on the lake just swarming with bullheads. My homemade fish spear worked well. Ed Sr. chuckled every time I speared a bullhead. "I was pretty skeptical about your spear but it worked pretty good after all," he told me as we closed the jeep doors.

And now here I was, back at home with my brother and four sisters, showing them how to clean a dozen fat bullheads. It was fun teaching them what I knew. Later on that evening Mom broiled the fish with butter, salt and pepper. They were delicious.

FIFTEEN

The floor above my room creaked as footsteps made their way across the hallway and into the kitchen. I heard the cupboard doors open. In the morning silence, Mom was upstairs in the kitchen looking for coffee and filters. It was around 6:00 a.m. and the thought of going to school really sucked. I was in bed half asleep and I knew the usual routine. Footsteps found their way from the kitchen to the top of the stairs, the door opened, "Get up and get ready for school!" Mom shouted. "Alright," I answered hesitantly, not wanting to leave the confines of my Coleman sleeping bag which I used instead of blankets. Ahh, might as well get up. I already stayed home once this week; I don't think another day will go over too well.

On the other side of the basement I could hear my brother Jimmy getting things together himself. Then, like clockwork, Dad came down and stoked the woodstove. 'Old Man Winter' had nearly reached its end, yet the stove's warmth kept the damp chill out of the air.

Not too hungry, I made a couple pieces of toast with honey on them, poured a cup of black coffee from the Mr. Coffee machine, and sat at the kitchen table with my math book and folder. Jackie, Annette and Sherry were eating Cheerios, talking amongst each other. Kristie was still in bed. With honey on each bite of toast, the coffee didn't need any sweetener. I ate quickly, put the cup and dish in the sink, then went to my room in search of a pencil. With no success, I went into Jimmy's room. There's gotta be a pencil somewhere, I thought. Right then I saw the folding slingshot next to Ben's empty cage. By now everyone was upstairs. Dad would be going to work and my brother and sisters to school. With a change of plans, I anxiously folded the slingshot, put it in my coat pocket then took off. Today was going to be fun.

I sat through English, history, then math, while getting side-tracked with thoughts of the slingshot. I'd forgotten my homework, math book and pencil, but my brother's slingshot was still in my coat pocket, and I knew just what I was going to do. The hour dragged on as I sat at the desk, empty handed, hoping the teacher wouldn't notice. Then, saved by the bell, it was lunch time. Pizza was on the menu. I hurried to the cafeteria, put my lunch ticket down and had myself a nice big slab—the school's pizza was some of the best.

Next thing I know, I'm downtown, underneath Lake Avenue's highway ramp, walking along the railroad tracks. The steel rails were rusted on the sides but almost chrome-like on top where the box cars' big heavy steel wheels rode. In between the wooden ties lay hundreds of taconite pellets that fell from the rumbling box cars.

It was warmer down here next to big Lake Superior and all the snow had melted. The rich aroma of coffee beans roasting filled the air. Not too far away was the ARCO coffee mill. I'd been here before on my journeys away from school and knew just the place where many pigeons lived. On my way I would step upon each wooden tie or walk the steel rail like it was a balancing beam, falling off then getting back on to try again. There were many empty box cars lined up on the tracks. Their big side doors were open; how many hobos rode these rails back in the Depression and do they still today, I wondered.

One afternoon while in Ely, Ed and I put a dozen pennies on the rails. The next morning they were flattened oblong and almost paper thin from the trains' massive weight. Reaching the spot, I looked up. Pigeons flew in and out underneath the busy roadway. I got closer, taking the slingshot from my pocket and unfolding it. There stood a big fat pigeon, bluish gray in color on a steel beam about 20 feet up. Reaching down but still keeping my eyes on the bird, I picked up a few marble-size taconite pellets from the track. I shot several times and missed. The pigeon just sat there without a flinch. I took aim again. This time more carefully and released the leather pouch from my thumb and forefinger…whapp…the pellet struck the bird in the breast. It fell, spinning end over end with one wing outward, then hit the ground.

I ran over; the bird didn't even twitch. The wrist rocket worked great. I once read an article in *Field and Stream* magazine, claiming pigeons were excellent table fare—it's called 'squab.' I decided to bring the bird home and see for myself. I went back up the hill in time to catch my ride home. The girls on the school bus thought I was disgusting when I showed them the bird, but that was part of the fun.

Hunting the pigeon down in the city was exciting but with the traffic and buildings everywhere, it just didn't feel right. Now, with the meat in the freezer, I could relax in the peaceful refuge of my room. I hung the rabbit hides that I dried earlier that week on the wall, then sat at my desk, sorting through the bullet collection my Uncle Louie gave me.

The three rabbit hides I had stretched earlier that week appeared to be dry now. I removed the small nails that held them to the plywood. Picking the two best, I looked around my room. Where should I put them—the gun rack? They would look great around the gun rack, I thought. I held them at many angles. After deciding which way would look best, I put them in their place. I stood back; they looked great hanging next to each other above my guns. Jimmy wasn't home from school yet so I put the wrist rocket back where I found it, next to Ben's cage.

While going back to my room, I ran into Mom at the bottom of the stairs. She had a basket full of laundry that needed washing. "Oh, you startled me!" she shrieked, with a surprised look on her face.

"I didn't mean to."

"We're going to have a surprise visitor tonight," she said while putting the clothes in the wash machine.

"Who?"

"You kids will just have to wait and see."

"Alright."

Underneath my bed I had a metal ammunition box. I grabbed it and sat at the edge of my bed. Inside there were many cartridges of different caliber. I opened the box, dumping them carefully on my bed. Their brass cases stood out against my green Coleman sleeping bag. Uncle Louie had a giant collection of many different kinds of bullets. When I showed my interest in being a collector, he had given these to me, along with a thick book, *Cartridges of the World.* I found it very interesting. The book described every round of ammunition ever made and what type of game they were effective on. I would sit there looking at each cartridge, one by one, day dreaming about rifles, pistols and the hunts I would love to go on, from as small as rabbits to as large as bears and elephants.

I was in the darkest continent of Africa, hunting the dangerous Cape buffalo. My weapon of choice—a bolt action rifle chambered in 458 Winchester magnum. I took aim behind the huge beast's shoulder. It turned its head, staring at me. I've got to shoot before it charges. Right when I went to take the shot…

Slam! The lid on the laundry machine closed, startling me, and the click, click, click of Mom turning the dial to get the load started. Darn it, my fantasy hunting trip was interrupted. I put the bullet collection back in the box carefully as to not damage them. I went upstairs to the living room with the rest of my family waiting anxiously for our surprise visitor. Getting up, Mom walked towards the kitchen, "I should get that water boiling," she said.

"Why are you boiling water?" I asked.

"We're having raviolis tonight."

Mmmmm…I can't wait. Homemade raviolis stuffed with cheese and Italian sausage smothered with my mom's special rich pasta sauce, I thought. Looking out the big front window, we saw a car pull up. It stopped, there was movement inside then the door opened. The person inside got out with a black guitar case in hand. It was our surprise visitor, Uncle Tommy!

"Jane Francis, your brother Tommy is here!" Dad shouted to Mom. All of us greeted our uncle as he came to the door. It had been a couple of years since we last saw him. After catching up briefly, he opened the black case.

"I've been practicing with this new guitar," he told us, "Thought I would play a couple of tunes for ya." Next to the kitchen's entry way, Tommy rested his back against the wall, strumming a few notes on his guitar. "Any suggestions?" he asked.

We were undecided. Mom got her new John Denver album. "Do you think you could play a few of these songs?" she asked.

"I'll give it my best, Janie."

Fifteen minutes later, we were all having a good time. After several songs, Mom looked at the back of the album. "Here, try this one, it's one of my favorites," she said happily.

After the first few notes, I recognized the tune, "Sunshine on my Shoulders." As Uncle Tommy played, I noticed the sun was shining through the front window and sparkling water dripped from the roof top.

SIXTEEN 🌿

Today had been a long time in the waiting… the snow had melted. All around, the woods seemed bare except for the plump green buds sprouting out of almost every tree branch. They looked almost fluorescent in the sunlight. Frogs croaked, lakes thawed, rivers and creeks flowed freely. Winter had released its icy grip. Spring was finally here and it was fishing opener.

My family and I were up on Island Lake. We'd set up for the morning, close to the dam. The shoreline was gravelly and the water dark, almost the color of tea. From his minnow bucket, Dad helped my sisters bait their lines with the squiggly sucker minnows we'd gotten from the bait shop and showed them where to cast. Mom was watching Kristie and making sandwiches from our Coleman cooler. Jim and I anxiously looked through our long awaiting tackle boxes.

"I think I'm gonna try a Mepps Bucktail lure, how about you?" I asked my brother.

"I'll give this purple rubber leech a try."

Getting closer to the water, we saw big suckers in the shallow areas spawning. We let them go about their business and cast our lures. By now my sisters' lines were out with their big red and white bobbers floating. Dad cast his yellow Fenwick rod with an open face reel and waited patiently with a sucker for bait; he preferred not to use a bobber.

We'd been there a while. Mom was pouring hot coffee for Dad and orange juice for the rest of us. Gathering around the big green cooler, we ate doughnuts, washing them down with the orange juice.

"Did ya see those suckers—they're pretty big? Dad asked.

"Yea, there's a bunch of them where Jimmy and I were. How are you going to know if you're getting a bite with no bobber?" I asked Dad curiously.

"I watch the line closely. When it starts to tighten up and the slack is gone, then I know."

"My bobber went down!" Annette shouted, running over excitedly, she reeled in. It was a small Northern.

"Hammer-handle," Dad joked. "Better put 'em back in the drink."

"Oh darn, I thought it would be bigger," Annette sighed while letting the small pike go.

About now I was fired up and ready to catch something. "I think you guys should use minnows," Dad suggested to Jimmy and I, since we were having no luck with our lures. I wanted to fish but didn't have the patience to sit there with a minnow on my hook. I wasn't picky when it came to fish. I'd take anything home—perch, bullheads, sunfish, catfish, suckers…wait a minute…the suckers. I had an idea. There were plenty of lures in my tackle box with treble hooks. I'll just take a set of them off. Removing the Bucktail lure I tied on a treble, it seemed light to cast. I had some large splitshot—that'll do the trick, I thought and clamped four of them right above the hook. It cast perfect. I let it sink where the suckers would swim by and waited. Within a couple of minutes they were back, twenty or more swam over the hook. I pulled the rod's tip back as if setting a hook on a fish. It worked! I pulled in a good sized one.

"I'm gonna try that!" Jimmy shouted.

Dad saw what we were up to, "Okay you guys, it's illegal to snag fish! You'd better stop before the Game Warden shows up!"

"They're only suckers, it will be okay," I answered. Not knowing myself if it was okay or not—I just hoped the Game Warden didn't show up

"If the Game Warden shows up, I don't want anything to do with it," he told us.

In a while, my brother and I had several suckers a piece. Our fish scale weighed them from 5 to 7 pounds. We were happy because we had fish to take home. Jim and I walked over on top of the dam. Water rushed out the back side with a loud roar into the Cloquet River. While Jim stood by the railing watching, I went to the other side. Looking down, I saw a huge beaver swimming. With a flap of its tail, it dove disappearing into the dark water. A funny thought crossed my mind—I bet the beaver thought he had the biggest dam in the territory.

Dad caught three good sized Northerns, all keepers and were on his stringer. "I think the fish are done biting for the day. Maybe we'll eat lunch and pack it up," Dad said. It looked like Jackie, Annette and Sherry were having fun walking the shoreline, collecting agates with Mom and Kristie. The styrofoam cups that held orange juice were now almost full of the colorful stones.

With the day still young and the morning catch cleaned, I found myself at the laundry room sink rinsing scales from my Rapala fillet knife. Mom was digging through the big chest freezer, "Hmmmm.. what sounds good?" she asked herself. I heard frozen packages being moved around. "Hey, I still have some cookies left; that's funny—I thought they were all gone. I think I'm going to make a nice cup of hot tea and relax," she remarked contentedly. Closing the freezer door, she went back upstairs with cookies in hand. I put the fillet knife in its leather sheath and back in the tackle box.

My bedroom window was half open. I could hear robins singing outside. They were back and nesting; a sure sign of spring. Sliding the tackle box underneath and next to the bullet collection box, I laid down on my bed with both hands behind my head. Both salamanders had gotten white spots all over their skin and died off. From my bed, I could see their empty home still sitting on the desk. No sooner had I laid down and I was up again, looking into the cooler. Their stone still sat in the bottom and the water almost all evaporated. Feeling bad for the small lizard-like creatures that once occupied my room, I went over to see Jimmy's new hermit crabs. He'd gotten a small aquarium and there they were on his desk where Ben had lived.

"Where did you find these things?" I asked.

"They had them up at the pet shop."

"I knew you'd find something sooner or later," I told him.

Right then Jimmy was sitting on the edge of his bed tossing a small blue bean bag he had made into the air and catching it. Wanting to get a closer look at a crab, I reached into the aquarium, picking one up by its bluish colored shell. I could see the tips of its legs barely sticking out. Why would someone want one of these, I thought. I looked even closer. Suddenly all the crab's legs sprang from its shell, startling me. I'd never seen one before; it looked kind of like a big spider.

"Pretty cool, huh?"

"Yea, how much were they?"

"Two bucks a piece."

"Cool!" I set it back in the aquarium's gravelly bottom. It was about then both of us heard Mom scream. Not knowing what was wrong, I took off and ran up the basement stairs. Jimmy followed. In no time we were at the kitchen table. Then my sisters and dad showed up, "What's wrong?"

"Who in the sam heck put the rat in the freezer? I almost had a heart attack!" Mom shouted, not looking happy. "That wasn't a very nice joke." My brother and I knew right away. I walked over and looked at the coffee can next to the steamy cup of tea. Sure enough—inside the pillow stuffing there was Jimmy's rat, Ben. His tail and back legs were sticking out of the top, frozen solid.

"We weren't playing a joke," Jimmy said. "Ben died awhile ago and we put him in the freezer so we could bury him in the summer." Relieved that Mom was in no danger, our family went about their business. Dad walked away shaking his head, "You boys get that rat outside and bury it." With that said, my brother put the lid on the can and we went back downstairs.

SEVENTEEN ✤

In full bloom, hundreds of dandelions filled the backyard. Their yellow tops were bright against the green carpeted grass. In the springtime, the dandelions' tender leaves taste great with vinegar and oil. A patch of wild onions grew behind the tin shed. Their strong (pungent) scent lingered in the air, which reminded me of a funny story…

When Aunt Kate and Mom were kids they had a milking cow named April. Often times she would roam outside the fenced-in area and nibble the tops off of the wild onions. On one occasion, it made her milk taste awful and it ended up down the kitchen sink drain.

Soon it would be time for my family and I to till up and plant, I thought while strolling past the garden's brown soil. One fall day we harvested squash. It was a good season and many grew huge. After picking them, Mom dropped a 22-pounder down the basement stairs. It bounced its way all the way down to the bottom and didn't even crack open.

It makes me wonder...you plant all these small seeds in the ground and it's like free food comes up.

Deciding to bury Ben for my brother, I had the coffee can in hand and headed towards the swamp. Frogs were croaking, a couple of red-winged blackbirds perched themselves on a cluster of pussy willows, making their familiar noises as they stretched their wings. The big yellow petals of cowslips opened up on the pond's smooth watery surface.

I crossed on the log that led to my fort. I hadn't been down here for a while and wanted to see how it made it through the winter. Upon reaching the area I noticed the four cedar trees which once held my shack were now bare except for a couple of boards that made up the floor. Someone or a couple of people had torn it down. This really sucks, I thought while looking at the plywood and parts of my stove scattered about. Maybe I'll put it back up this summer, not today though. A little discouraged, I left, looking for a place to put Ben. I wonder what ever happened to Thumper, Jackie's pet rabbit. Not too long ago she let him loose so he'd be free. He was huge, grayish white, with large feet. That's why she named him Thumper. I never did see him again. I hoped he survived. Jackie sure missed him.

Crossing over to the field where those sumacs grew, I found a spot. Next to some tall maples was a small tree stump. I took Ben from the can, setting him on the flat surface. It looked like he was just resting there in the woods. This is good, I thought to myself.

Great Grandpa Frank lived above us. His house was simple. It was basically a one-room deer shack with a wood stove to heat the place, kerosene lanterns for light, and a root cellar for storing vegetables. There was no electricity. His diet was also simple; he had oatmeal every day for breakfast and salt pork. During the Depression when meat was hard to come by, he would make lard sandwiches. Aunt Kate told me one of his favorite snacks was piping hot coffee with an egg cracked in it. Out back behind the shack were eight cords of split birch with a small creek running behind it. For water, he'd go in these woods with glass apple cider jugs and get his drinking water from a spring way down in the cedar swamp. Even on hot days the water ran cool. Great Grandpa had passed away but the well he had discovered still flows. Sometimes there would be little shiner minnows swimming in the crystal clear water... I think I'll go check it out.

It was beautiful out; one of those days where it was just a little cool but the sun warmed your clothes, keeping you comfortable. I'd almost reached the area when I heard some leaves ruffling. Looking to my left there were six baby foxes trampling about. I walked over to get a closer look—maybe I could catch one. As I approached, they all scurried into that hole I noticed during winter. These would be the coolest pets. Surely nobody in the neighborhood had one of these—I was going to be the first.

In no time I was almost back home. I'd chucked Ben's coffee can in the scrap pile behind the oak tree and was now in the tin shed looking for a shovel. Hmmm... let's see here—a couple of rakes, a pitch fork we used for digging up potatoes, a snow shovel, which of course wouldn't be good for digging up dirt. Ohhh, my homemade ice chisel I made in shop class for ice fishing, a couple of hoes... ahhh here we go. I set the shovel outside the shed. Excited to share my find, I ran into the house and made a phone call to my friend Ed across the street.

By now bread pans of rising dough sat on the kitchen counter. Mmmm... fresh bread tonight, I thought. In no time here comes Ed down their steep driveway and across the street.

"Where are they?"

"I'll show you." I grabbed the shovel and we were off. "Yea, these are going to make the coolest pets."

"Can I have one, too?" Ed asked.

"Yea, let's see how many there are."

Back at the site, we took turns digging. The hole tunneled

inward about seven feet.

"Man, are you sure there is anything in here?"

"I'm sure, just wait."

After a couple more shovels of dirt, there they were—five baby red foxes looking at us curiously. Ed picked one up, "Hey there little guy." Ed tucked two inside his jean jacket and I put the other three in my wind breaker.

Back home under the back porch, I had a good size live trap about four feet long and two feet square I used for catching stray cats, raccoons, and skunks just for fun, and then I would let them go.

"What are you doing?" Ed asked as I lifted the flap on one end.

"I'm gonna keep my foxes in here."

"Hmm, I just want one."

I placed the three I had carried back into the cage-like trap.

"Here, have this one, too."

I took the fox carefully from Ed's hands, placing it with the others. They walked around in their bare but new home.

"I'm gonna have to line the bottom with some of that tall grass growing behind the oak tree."

In both hands, Ed held the nervous baby fox, "I've got a big cardboard box up in our garage. I'm gonna run home and fix a place for mine."

"OK, talk to you later." I moved the cage onto the flat sidewalk just outside the basement door.

"Cool, where did you get those?" Jimmy asked while stepping outside.

"I found them in the woods. They'll make cool pets, huh?"

"Yea."

"I gotta go back and get the shovel. Come with and I'll show you where I found them." We just passed the oak tree. "Yea, I was just back in the woods and I saw these foxes. I tried to catch one but they ran back into their den, so me and Ed came back and dug 'em out."

"Can I have one, too?"

Back near the hole I knelt down and grabbed the shovel.

77

Looking through where we dug, Jimmy shouts, "There is still one in here!"

"Really? There you go then, you can have that one," I told him.

"Cool."

"Let's get out of here."

On our way home, I picked a bunch of field grass and put a good layer inside the live trap. Five foxes total now. They must be hungry. I went into the kitchen and put some milk in a cereal bowl.

"What are you guys doing?" Dad asked while I warmed the milk up in the microwave.

"We've got some baby foxes outside."

"You don't want to get caught with them," Dad said with a raised voice. "The Game Warden finds you with them, there will be a fine to pay."

"I just want them for pets." No one had to know.

My brother and I watched as the foxes eagerly lapped up the milk. I bet they will eat canned dog food. It's soft and should be easy for them to chew, I thought. It was later in the day now, starting to cloud up and it looked like we were in for some heavy rain.

"Let's bring these foxes inside so they don't get cold and wet."

"Where should we put them?"

"Next to the furnace between the two rooms. Then they will stay warm," I told my brother.

Mom was in need of a few items from the grocery store. She had picked up her supplies and was now back. Jim and I ran upstairs.

"Did you get some dog food?" we asked.

"Yes, I picked up a couple of cans."

I reached into the grocery bag and there they were – two cans.

"Thanks."

"That's OK for now but I can't afford to be feeding a bunch of foxes every day."

"I know. Me and Jim will take care of it," I assured her. I opened the flap, setting a small saucer with half a can of moist dog food inside of the cage. All five foxes crowded, nudging each other trying to find their spot; their tongues and teeth smacking up the food. My brother and I watched contentedly.

The phone rang. Ed was on the phone. "My fox keeps whining. It won't stop; I think it's lonely. Can I have another one to put with him so he will stop?"

"Maybe it is too cold in the garage."

"Yea, maybe," Ed said. "If he keeps whining I will come and bring him back so he can be with the others."

"Our foxes are eating dog food right now."

"Really?" Mine won't eat or drink."

"OK, well, I guess we will talk tomorrow."

After getting off the phone, Jim and I covered the cage with a blanket. "Well, we should get some rest."

"Yea, I'm tired," answered Jimmy. Soon the foxes, Jimmy and I were sound asleep.

School was finally out and summer on its way. The foxes were quite bigger now, almost half grown. Our parents didn't like the strong smell of fox urine in our room and Ed's parents didn't like the idea of having a whining fox in the garage. So now next to the garden, all six of them were in a cage my brother and I had made from some leftover chicken wire. They seemed friendly and would follow us everywhere in the backyard. We'd grown very attached to our fuzzy brownish pets, which were now almost fully red and more mature looking. Their diet of canned dog food and blackbirds I'd gotten with a BB gun was doing the trick.

They were really cool but at the rate the foxes were eating, I would have no money left to fill the tank on our Yamaha 80 Dad had bought Jimmy and I—**and we liked to ride**. All of our friends had a dirt bike of one kind or another. It seemed like nothing else mattered during the summer months, except of course for fishing.

Once we left the backyard, that was it—we were gone all day. There were trails everywhere. One of our favorite spots was a big deep pond up by the airport. We called it 'Airbase Pond.' On hot days, everyone would go swimming or just sit back and watch planes go by overhead. There were many different kinds; big jet airliners, small two-seaters and, my favorite—jet fighters. When they took off you could see flames coming out the back and the pilot with his helmet on inside the cockpit.

Sunfish and bullheads lived in the pond. One summer day while we were fishing for them a small frog hopped by. Jimmy decided to try something different. Catching the frog, he tied on a big hook.

"What are you doing?" I asked.

"See if I can catch anything using this for bait."

"You're never gonna catch anything with that. There's nothing big enough in here," I told him as he cast.

The big red bobber plopped, leaving ripples on the water's calm surface. Deciding to take a break, I noticed an empty box someone had discarded in the tall weeds. There were frogs everywhere. One by one I placed the tiny green black spotted leopard frogs into the empty twelve pack container. My brother was gone. His pole sat there propped up with a 'Y' shaped stick poked into the sandy shoreline.

Some light fog rolled in and was now getting thicker. It looked like our sunny afternoon was going to turn into rain. It had been a half hour or so; there must have been a few dozen frogs in the box by now. "That's enough," I said to myself.

"Look what I caught!" I heard Jimmy say. Here comes my brother carrying a big mud turtle.

"What are you going to do with that?" I asked curiously.

"I don't know. Maybe I'll take it home," he said, grinning from ear to ear.

Walking over to the sandy shoreline, I set the frogs free. As they hopped away I counted thirty-eight in all.

"What did you catch all them for?"

"There were so many. I thought it would be fun," I told my brother. "You should let the turtle go; we've got to get going."

While Jimmy was making up his mind, I started reeling in his line. Suddenly there was a huge splash. "Did you see that?" We were both in awe as a big northern pike snapped the ten pound test fishing line. "I never knew there were northerns in here!" I shouted.

It would sure be nice to take a ride up to the pond but not today. Our dirt bike was in the motorcycle shop in need of a new piston and rings. Dad wasn't too happy about that. He'd used his bonus check to buy the dirt bike and now this costly repair.

Feeling kind of sick, (my brother and I thought we contracted rabies from the foxes) we needed a break from them and we were now behind the oak tree plinking away at bottles and cans with our new pump-up Crossman air rifles—a big step up from my Daisy BB gun. Now I'd have a pellet gun with enough power to bag rabbits, partridge, the big gray squirrels in our backyard, and other small game, I thought as every shot zipped through both sides of the tin can. We got a good bargain with our hard earned money we'd saved. The air rifles could fire lead pellets or BB's. A carton of 800 golden BB's didn't cost much and would last a few days of shooting, which was fine by me. Yep… pet foxes, new pellet gun… what more cold you ask for… life was great.

It seems to me you really know you're in trouble when your parents don't say a word. It wasn't too much longer I saw Dad marching down the backyard. Usually if he wanted our attention he would yell from the back porch, and here he was about fifteen feet away and getting closer.

"Set them pellet guns down," he mumbled. "You've got company. How many times did I tell you?"

"What?" I asked.

"About getting in trouble with the Game Warden. I told you and I told you I don't want anything to do with it. If there's a fine, don't look at me," he said in a stern voice.

Nervously I walked back up to the house. I looked up and there he was—the same Game Warden that shot the big bear. I felt hotter than usual as perspiration dampened my flannel shirt.

"I understand you have some pets down there."

"What do you mean?" I asked.

"I mean word in the neighborhood says you got about six foxes. Did you know it's against the law to keep a wild animal caged up?"

Playing dumb, which seemed to work from time to time, "No, I didn't know that. When did they make up that law? I just saw them walking around and took them home." No way on God's green earth was I gonna tell him I took a shovel and dug them from their den.

81

"Looks like we have a trip to make."

"Where?" I asked.

"I could have you arrested for having these foxes in your possession."

"Well, we were just gonna keep them for a while and let them go," I told him, hoping that would get me off the hook. He noticed the live trap now, sitting under Mom's clothesline pole.

Now here I was, six foxes inside the live trap and me, in the Game Warden's car. A trip to the county jail didn't set well with me as I looked out the front window with despair at my family. Starting the car, the Game Warden backed up. I had a huge knot in my stomach. Suddenly the car stopped, "I'll tell you what—since it's your first offense I'm gonna pretend this visit never happened. But don't let me come back and find something like this out again."

"That's a deal," I reassured him.

The Game Warden backed out of the driveway. I was finally relieved when the car's rooftop disappeared over the hill. Nothing sounds better to me right now than to be at a lake waiting for my red and white bobber to go under.

Jeff and Jimmy with the baby foxes.

EIGHTEEN

It was a quiet day, there wasn't much going on around the house and I needed something to do. I remembered earlier that week Irvin stopped by for coffee and told my parents and I about the problem he was having with squirrels. It was then that I decided to go have a look.

My brother Jimmy looked like he was pretty bored too, so I asked him if he wanted to come with me. "Yeah! There's nothing to do around here!" he said with excitement. After telling him about the squirrel problem, we grabbed our new pellet guns and took off.

About halfway there we stopped for a minute to catch our breath. Reaching into his windbreaker pocket, Jim pulled out a bag of trail mix and took a handful. "Want some?" he asked. "Yeah, looks good," I said as I poured some out in my hand. Then chewing it up, we started down the road towards Irvin's house.

It wasn't too much further when I noticed one of the neighbors had a go-kart for sale. We walked over to the front yard to check it out. It was a two-seater with a seven and a half horse engine on the back. The frame was red with a black seat and it had a chrome steering wheel.

After looking it over we started back down the road. The 'For Sale' sign said $85, I knew there wasn't that much in my wallet, and I wanted so much to take the two-seater for a ride. I just had to find a way to get the rest of the money, I thought to myself.

As Jimmy and I were walking, we talked about how much fun it would be to drive around trails. That made me want it even more, so finally I said with determination, "That's it. I'm going to own that go-cart."

"Where are you gonna get the money?"

"I don't know, but I'll find a way."

About then we reached Irvin's road. It was a nice day and once again there was the old man sitting down with his cane, enjoying the sunshine. When we got closer to the stone wall, I said, "Nice day out," to the old gentleman. He looked up from his crouched position with a big smile and eyes sparkling, "Yup, good as it gets…good as it gets." Then he was silent. Again, I could see he was happy that I said "Hi" to him. I was too, but sad at the same time thinking how lonely he must be. It was sure nice to know that he made it through one of our long Minnesota winters.

Walking by, we passed the big apple tree, which was now in full bloom with its pinkish blossoms, giving off their flowery fragrance and bees pollinating them.

"Smells good," Jimmy said.

"Yeah, so are the apples." And a little further was the sweet corn garden with its new sprouts coming up. Then down the driveway we went. Irvin was in the garage section of the barn with one of his many friends.

"Hey Jeff!" he shouted, "How would you and Jimmy like to watch us patch up a tractor tire?"

"OK!" kind of shouting back, because he had poor hearing.

When we reached the big sliding barn door and went in, Irvin introduced us to his friend, Leo.

"Hello," he said busily as he slid the floor jack under the rear axle and raised the big tire.

"I see you guys brought your pellet guns over," Irvin said, wiping the grease from his hands with an old blue rag.

"Yeah, we came over to shoot some squirrels for ya," I replied.

"Well, why don't you watch us fix this tire and learn something? I finally got a chance to work on it, being that I was so busy plowing this winter."

I agreed, leaning the pellet gun next to the garage door. There were a lot of old junk cars and trucks parked out in the field, so Jim took his pellet gun and walked behind the barn to have a look at them, while I stayed in the garage. Having removed the lug nuts earlier, the tire and rim were ready to come off. "Well," Irvin said, stretching his arms up in the air, "let's get going and fix this thing." Then all three of us got a good grip.

"On the count of three we'll go, all right?" Leo said anxiously. "Ready…one…two…three, go!" Pulling and lifting the tire from the tractor we laid it down on the oil stained garage floor. Irvin sat down on the edge, removing the stopper from the valve stem. All of a sudden, we heard 'pfffffsssss' as the air started rushing out.

"It takes a long time to drain out one of these tractor tires," Irvin said, while the rubbery smelling air was still pouring out.

"I bet it does," I replied curiously, with the go-kart still on my mind.

I told Irvin about the go-kart.

"What do you want a go-kart for? Nope. Save your money for something practical. You should buy a tractor, then you can have a big garden and grow your own food. That's what I would do if I were you." I sure didn't want a tractor and, with respect, I wasn't going to tell him that. Then he and Leo started talking, so I decided to walk out in the back field.

Jimmy had set his pellet gun on the hood of an old red and white Chevy station wagon. He was in the driver's seat, making engine and squealing noises imagining he was a race car driver. I'm sure he wasn't bored, but just in case I went over an asked him to check things out with us.

When we walked back into the garage, Irvin was fumbling through the workshop drawers, saying to himself calmly, "I know they're in here somewhere."

"What are you looking for?" Jimmy asked.

"Tire patches. I'll find them, there in here somewhere."

About then, trying to help, Jim was looking in one of the drawers where he stumbled upon a box.

Curious to see what was in it, he opened the box and inside was a Johnson fishing reel. It had been sitting in the drawer for many years, but it still looked brand new. Excitedly, he took it from the box; "Can I have it?" Jim asked.

Irvin picked up the fishing reel and looked at it. "Sure, go ahead, it's been sitting in here a long time. I'll never use it. Well, I can't find the patches, I guess I'll have to go to the store and pick some up. Hey, boys, it's getting late, why don't you call headquarters and tell your mom that I'll be driving you home."

NINETEEN

I couldn't get the go-kart off of my mind, so I called my friend Dan and told him about it. "Sounds cool," he told me, "We had roast beef last night so I'm going to make a sandwich and I'll be right over." I explained to him which neighbor was selling the go-kart and we decided to meet there. Anxious to go see it again, we said "Good-bye." As soon as I hung up the phone I was on my way.

I was hoping I got there fast enough so nobody else would buy it. About half way there, I reached the top of the hill. I felt my heart drop. It was gone! With a sick feeling in my stomach, I continued towards the house. I could see the 'For Sale' sign was still laying in the yard. About then, Dan walked over. "We're too late," I said.

"That's a bummer," he said, disappointed. All of a sudden, the garage door opened. There it was! Glad to see no one bought it! We walked over and asked the guy what he was doing.

"Well, the tires needed some air, but they're full now," he "So, you want $85?" I asked.

"That's what I would like to get."

"Will you let us take a test drive?" Dan asked.

"Sure, if you're serious about buying it," the man told us, kind of frustrated. "Yeah, just yesterday I let someone do that and wouldn't ya know it, after an hour he brought the damn thing back."

"Really?" Dan asked.

"Yeah, looks like the kid took it all over hell's creation. That's why the front bumper is bent in. No, boys, I'm not going through that again. Show me some green or I'll take something for trade," he said, scratching his head.

Dan and I talked it over. "Guess what," Dan said, "I've got $40 on me." Yeah and I'm broke I thought to myself—wait a second, I still have that old .22 rifle I fixed up last fall. Forty dollars and the gun should be an even trade. I wasn't sure that I wanted to part with the gun so I didn't mention the idea.

One thing was for sure, we wanted the go-cart, and to show that we were serious, Dan let the guy hold onto his money. Both of us sat down, Dan in the driver's side.

"OK, guys, ready?" the man asked.

"Yep."

He pulled the rope; the engine fired and came to an idle.

"Go ahead!" He was shouting over the noisy engine.

Excited and smiling, we took off down the dead end street, which was bumpy and full of potholes. With every bump, the go-cart rattled. There was no suspension and it took the bumps pretty hard, but we were having too much fun to let that bother us anyway. After going three blocks, we reached the end of the road and pulled over. "You gotta try this!" Dan said,

"It's a blast!" Anxiously, we switched seats.

Ahead of us was a big field, with trails everywhere. I stepped on the gas pedal and the tires spun out on the gravely ground. We went even faster until we hit the rutted-out trail and had to slow down. We saw some friends on their dirt bikes and drove over to them.

"Where did you get that?" one of them asked.

"It was for sale up the street and we're taking it for a test drive," I told him.

"I'll tell you what, if you're not interested, I think I'll check it out," another said. With that, I told them I had things to do and left.

I remembered the man saying that he would take something for trade, so I hurried and got to the other side of the field. Crossing the street, we pulled into the front yard of my house.

"What are you doing?" Dan asked.

"Wait a minute. I'll be right back."

In a hurry, I ran to the basement door and went into my bedroom. There it was—the 22 rifle I fixed up last fall. The go-kart seemed to be so much fun and I wanted to drive it a lot more. So reaching up, I took the rifle from the gun rack, looked at it one more time and slid it into the case.

I thought the man would be upset by now so, not wasting any time, I ran back to the go-kart.

"What's with the gun case?" Dan asked.

"Remember he said that he would take something for trade."

"Aah! That's right."

"This .22 should take care of the other half."

"Cool! 'Cause I don't have the rest of the money!"

"We'd better get back there so he's not angry."

"We're outta here!"

Finally, at the top of the hill, we could see him standing there, waiting for us. We came to a stop. "I thought you guys took off for sure," he said, calmly.

"Remember you said you would take something for trade?" I asked him, taking the rifle out of the case, "How about this, plus the forty dollars?"

Holding the rifle, he opened the bolt and looked down the barrel, "You got yourself a deal!"

TWENTY

In Dan's backyard, behind the garage, we were looking at the go-kart. We were anxious to drive it somewhere. It was pretty beat up and needed some work. Next to the garage were a couple rows of unsplit firewood.

Each grabbing a log, we stood them upright and sat down. A car pulled into the driveway. The doors slammed. Dan's brother Randy walked towards us.

"Look guys," he said, while holding up two of the biggest catfish I'd ever seen.

Both of us jumped up and asked, "Wow! Where did you get them?"

"I got them behind Walt's bar on the Cloquet River. "Yeah! I caught them last night on a big sucker minnow." With that said, he set his catch down in the shade and went into the house.

"Let's ask your brother if he'll take us to the river," I said, while looking at the huge catfish.

"OK, I'll see what he says."

The kitchen door opened with a loud creak. Randy walked

across the deck, hopped down the steps and went into the garage. He came back with pliers, knife, hammer, and two nails, and then he reached down and grabbed one of the fish. There was a tree nearby. He nailed the fish through the head to the tree's trunk. We watched as he slit the skin around the back of the head. Then, grabbing the pliers, he pulled the skin off. Before Randy started on the next fish, Dan cleared his throat, "We were wondering if you could take us up to the river?"

"Well, I would but I have to split some firewood today."

Everyone was busy so it looked like we were going nowhere. "We should just take the go-kart," I said jokingly.

"Yeah right."

"But it seems to run pretty good, just needs a little work done on it, and besides, there's nothing else to do."

"Ya think so?"

"Yes! Let's just go!" Laughing, we decided to give it a try. A few things needed to be done first.

Dan went into the garage and came back with his toolbox. I noticed the throttle cable was loose and adjusted it while Dan tightened up the brake pedal. Walking over with a garden hose, Randy started spraying the mess off the tree he had cleaned the fish on. "What are you guys up to?" he asked.

"We're going to take this thing up to the river," Dan said, while oiling the chain.

"Good luck—you'll need it." Randy took his cleaned fish into the house.

About then, the sky clouded up, and it started to sprinkle. "We're going to make it up there," I said, pushing the go-kart under the cover of the tall pine tree.

"Yeah, but we might end up pushing it all the way back home," Dan said.

"No, we won't. That's why we're fixing it."

"I hope so."

The engine ran smooth and had plenty of power, but from past experience with dirt bikes quitting on me and ruining a fun day, I had to check the spark plug. A few long walks home told me this. At first the plug wouldn't budge; I pulled harder on the wrench's handle. It broke free and came loose. The plug must have been in there a long time, I thought. After removing it, I could see there was a lot of carbon buildup. We didn't have any money for a new one so, making do; I cleaned up the old plug with a wire brush and put it back in.

"We're almost ready," I said.

"Yeah, we just need to fill the tank." Grabbing a gas can from the garage, Dan removed the gas cap and started pouring it in. "I love the smell of gasoline. There's just something about it."

"Me, too." Then after he put the cap back on, I pulled the rope; the engine fired on the first try and ran smoother than ever.

TWENTY-ONE

The journey was about to begin. We were determined to make it to the river. "I'll be right back—gottta get a couple of things from the basement." Dan said. While he was in the house, I went into the garage, put the tools back and grabbed some hand cleaner. He came back with two fishing poles; one of them didn't have a reel on it.

"How do you like these?" asked Dan as he handed a pole to me, the one without a reel. "These are really cool—where did you get them?"

"They used to be my dad's."

I never saw a pole like this—the whole rod was made of steel, from handle to tip. After wiping the cleaner from my hands, I threw the paper towel into the garbage. "Looks like we're all set. Let's just stop by my house on the way," I said. Dan jumped in the driver's side, while I went behind and pulled the rope. The engine started. I grabbed the two poles, set them in the middle of the seat between us and sat down. We headed out the driveway and down the road. We got to my house in no time at all. It was much faster than riding bikes—almost like owning a car, I thought.

"I'll be right back," I told Dan. As I opened the back door, the kitchen smelled of something good baking. On the table, there were dozens of chocolate chip cookies cooling off.

"What are you guys up to?" Mom asked.

"We're going to try catching some catfish up at Walt's River Inn," I said.

I walked through the kitchen and went down into my room. I just had to try that old fishing reel Irvin gave my brother, so I took that along with some fishing hooks and a box of sinkers, put them in my pocket and ran back upstairs.

"Can I have a few of these?" I asked, taking four of the cookies.

"Yeah, but they're still hot."

"That's good, they're better that way." Before she could ask how I was getting there, I hurried out the door, "See ya later!"

I sat down on the seat, "These are fresh baked," I said, handing Dan two of the soft cookies. Taking a bite, the warm chocolate tasted so good as it melted in my mouth.

"Mmmm," Dan said, "these are good."

"Yeah, just the right thing before we take off."

The sky was darker now and it was cool and windy. There was a chance for thunderstorms, but with the catfish on our minds, we were going to go anyway. Again, I went behind and started the engine. As I stood up, there was a big gust of cold air. The chill made me zip up my jacket. I sat down.

"Brrrr…It's cold out!" Dan said loudly over the sound of the engine.

"Yeah it is. Which way should we take?"

"I don't know for sure—let's just get going!"

Reaching the end of the driveway, I told Dan, "I know a short-cut."

So up the road we went, following its shoulder—feeling good that we found our own way. The road was freshly paved that spring so the ride was nice and smooth. We were almost a mile up the road when we had to slow down because there was a tow truck pulling a pickup out of the ditch. The traffic was busy that day so instead of going around the wrecker, we decided to watch for a few minutes. With its warning lights flashing, the man walked over and hooked the winches cable to the rear bumper then went back to the wrecker and pushed the lever. The cable tightened, slowly pulling the truck out of the muddy ditch. It was fun to watch and we didn't say much. Finally, the pickup was out. "I'll be out of your way in a minute," he said, jokingly. Then he jumped into his truck, shut off the hazard lights and took off. We were free to go again. This time, I wanted to drive so we switched sides.

There was a busy intersection about a half-mile down the road that I didn't want to go through. The short cut was just ahead of us. The road was clear so I decided to cross at that time. We were going pretty fast as I held it wide open. The faster we went, the colder the air felt. Once on the other side we got onto the dirt bike trail that ran next to Irvin's cornfield. I knew this was a good idea; it would save us a couple of blocks and avoid the intersection. Getting closer to the garden, we saw a fat woodchuck standing upright next to its hole. I should have brought my .22, I thought to myself.

The woodchuck scurried into its burrow as we went past. As we went a little further, we smelled something awful! "What's that smell?" Dan asked.

"I'm not sure."

In the distance, I could see Irvin on his tractor, turning the soil over in the garden. He didn't see us and we were in a hurry. We saw four huge piles of what looked like dirt. I drove over to see what it was. When we got there, the smell was just terrible. We both got off the go-kart to investigate, only to discover that it was chicken manure! Irvin was spreading it all over the garden for fertilizer. The smell was strong so we decided to leave right away.

For about two more blocks, there were giant weeping willows alongside the trail. I liked the way they looked with their long branches hanging towards the ground. Turning off to the side, I missed most of them, but from the earlier rain, the drenched leaves got us wet anyway. At the end, we reached the shoulder of the highway.

"I want to drive now," Dan told me. So switching sides, we continued onward—only this time, up the side of a major highway. The going was nice and smooth, except for that rattling sound of the go-kart frame when we would hit the bumps. As we went farther, a giant blue

Mac truck with all its chrome shining was heading our way. When it got closer, I could see the driver with his dark pilot glasses and full beard. He gave us the 'thumb's up' sign and blew the truck's loud air horn. As the tires rumbled passed, I thought of how easily they could crush us if we weren't careful.

The sign ahead of us said the speed limit was 50 mph. Even though we were going full speed, the traffic still passed us pretty quickly. "How fast do you think we're going?" Dan shouted over the noise of the go-kart's engine.

"What would you say—around 35?" I shouted back.

"Sounds about right to me."

Keeping up that speed, we were leaving the city behind and going farther into the country. Tired of shouting back and forth, we just sat back and kept driving.

About then, I saw the bait shop and remembered we had to get some sucker minnows. It must have been on Dan's mind, too, because he drove right into the parking lot. We stopped and killed the engine.

TWENTY-TWO

Finally at the river's edge, I stretched my arms and legs. It was a long drive and I was sore.

"Looks like a perfect day for fishing," I said.

"Yeah it does. Over there by all those rocks is where Randy caught the catfish," Dan told me.

I looked over; the river was wide with dark brownish colored water that flowed calmly except where it narrowed off and ran through the rocks making white foamy bubbles. It reminded me of pouring a glass of root beer over ice and watching the suds bubble over.

"I can't believe it, 26 miles and we're here," said Dan with amazement.

"Yeah, she ran perfect the whole way." Reaching down, I pulled the dipstick from the engine, wiping it off on my old blue jeans, put it back in and checked the oil level. "Cool, it didn't burn any oil either.

Let's see how much gas we burned up." Taking the cap off the tank I looked and surprisingly there was a little over half left.

"She gets good gas mileage, too," I said, smiling.

"The chain is holding up pretty good too—good that I oiled it well," Dan answered.

"Guess what."

"What?"

"Remember when we crossed the railroad tracks – how rough it was?"

"Yeah"

"Well, that was enough to crack the engine mounts," I showed him with a knot in my stomach.

"Ahhhh, we're still going to make it home—that's nothing," Dan said

"Yeah we will," I told him, though not really sure myself.

Trying not to let the cracked engine mounts get to me, I picked up the old fishing pole and took the reel from my coat pocket. It fit just right and looked great.

"Look at this."

"Cool, I like the way that it looks," Dan said, while getting his pole ready.

"Yeah, me too. Looks like my brother put some new line on the reel. This should work good."

The weather was fair, just a little cloudy. Since it was still daylight and catfish usually feed in the evening hours, I decided to tie on a daredevil spoon, a very popular fishing lure—red with a white stripe down the middle of it. While Dan got busy casting out different lures he brought, I decided to walk down stream and have a look. There was tall grass and weeds everywhere and since there was no trail along the bank of the river, I had to cut through them. They were really thick, almost jungle like, I thought pushing my way past their dampness. Just a little further and I'll be out of this mess. I got through okay, only soaking wet from head to toe. In the clearing, I discovered a big boulder next to the water's edge. This would be a good place to fish, I thought. It was warmer out and my shirt was uncomfortably wet, so I took it off, hanging it over a tree branch to dry. I stood on the big boulder, looking out over the river. There were weeds and lily pads everywhere along the whole shoreline—a perfect place for fish to hide out, I thought. I cast the rod hard, the daredevil sailed through the air, straight out in front of me and went far. 'Krrrr plunk' as it hit the water. I waited a few seconds for the lure to sink then started reeling it in amongst the heavy growth. All I caught was a clump of weeds. I took them off the treble hook and cast again, only this time not as far.

The daredevil landed right on top of a lily pad, when all of a sudden; there was a big swirl and splash. A huge northern pike had taken the bait. The fish was fighting hard almost bending the old pole in half. I let up the drag on the old reel so the taut line wouldn't break. The big fish jumped from the water, dancing on its tail.

Right then I heard a voice, "Looks like ya got a big one on." Standing behind me was a man with a long handled fishing net. "You keep on bringing that big boy in and I'll take my net to 'em," he said excitedly.

I kept reeling the pike in, keeping all slack from the fishing line.

"Yep, that's right, just bring 'em on in and I'll net 'er."

Almost to the boulder, the huge pike made one last lunge, trying to break free.

"Hold on! Hold on! I'll get 'em!" The man walked past the boulder into waist deep water, dipping the net. "I got 'em. Yes sa, he's a biggon and that's a fact!" The pike was thrashing back and forth in the net. "Yes sa, just look at the size of 'em. I bet he's a 14, mayba 15 pounda," bringing the fish to shore. He let it flop in the grass. "How's ya all doin' today. Yes sa, ma name's Taylor—L.C. Taylor, carpenter ba trade. Pleased to meet ya."

"My name's Jeff," I told him, while I was taking the daredevil out of the pike's mouth and picking it up by the gills.

"Well, Jeff, that's quite a fish. Ma famila's been camped out now for 'bout a week, mayba longa."

"Where?"

"Just ova here." We walked up the trail towards the campground.

I saw smoke and smelled a campfire. "We's here," the man told me. I noticed the large canvas tarp strung up overhead, protecting the campsite. "Jeff, this here's ma beloved wife Mabel and ma son of 12 years, Jacob Lee."

"Hi Jeff, welcome to our home," Mabel said with a smile.

"Hi Jeff," Jacob said.

I noticed Taylor had a strong southern accent. Curiously, I asked him where they were from.

"We all come up from Mississipp, bayou country, or so they say. Yes sa, been outta work fo sometime. Thought I'd give 'er a try up here. Nuthin' promisn' yet—just is' helpin' old Walt cook-n-wash dishes at the Inn. We'll make do—yes sa—I got me a good woman who loves me and a smart son doin' just fine in school," Taylor said proudly.

Jacob was barefoot with faded jeans and a straw hat. He had no belt; just a length of rope wrapped around and tied in a knot, and was happy as one could be. Mabel was busy—there was a fold out table with a camp stove and cooking utensils, along with flour, oil, and different spices.

"Just getting things ready for supper," she said, "We're gonna eat good today."

"Oh yeah? What's on the menu?" I asked.

"Looks to me like northern pike."

It was getting quite warm out and the chances of making it home without the big fish spoiling were slim at best. "Ya know that sounds good, and I suppose you mean the pike I just caught," I said jokingly.

"No, no, no, I didn't mean anything by it—just kiddin' round. That's your fish. Do with it as ya see fit," Mabel teased back.

"Well, well, well," Taylor joins in as he puts more wood on the smoldering fire, "Afta all me and ma trusta ol' net here helped land the big boy. Seems ta me ya wouldn't have gotten 'em in if it weren't for that fact. Yes sa, we sure is hungra and ma messes can cook good, yes sa."

"Okay, okay," I started laughing, "Whatta ya say Jacob, want some fish for supper?"

"Mmmmmm, sure I do," he replied, rubbing his belly and licking his lips.

"All right then,"Taylor said while taking the lid off a large coffee can.

To my surprise, there was no coffee, but hooks, sinkers, bobbers, and different fishing lures. Taylor dug through the tackle. "There she be," he said, taking out an old fillet knife.

"How come your fishing stuff's in that can?" I asked.

"Neva did own a fanca bait box, and when I open 'er up, evra things right there—easy ta grab. Yes sa, ya makes do with what ya got, and the good Lord will provide the rest."

Meanwhile, Mabel had set a week of newspapers on the table. "We can clean the fish on this," she said.

"Okay, that will work," I replied, laying the pike down.

Taylor was busy running the knife back and forth on a sharpening stone, "Gonna get 'er nice 'en sharp. It'll need it." Taylor walked over; all of us were standing around the table. "Jeff caught 'em, now I'm gonna clean 'em, that's only fair. Wouldn't ya say?"

"Yes, and I'll get the oil heated up so we're ready," Mabel told us anxiously.

"Jacob, you watch me now so's ya rememba how ta do this." Jacob and I watched as Taylor slit the pike's belly open. Inside were small sunfish, sucker minnows, and a few leeches. "This is how ya can figure what kinda bait ta use."

"Good to know," I answered back.

Then, running the blade behind the gills and down the spine, Taylor removed the fillets from both sides, setting the whitefish colored meat aside.

"Well son, now ya got a good idea. That's ha most fish is cleaned except catfish."

"I think I can do it," Jacob answered back.

Mabel came back over with a jug of water. I wrapped the fish head and guts in the paper while she rinsed off the fillets. "Where should I get rid of this?" I asked Taylor.

"Just chuck 'er in the fire."

I did and put some wood over the top, letting it burn up good.

"What time is it anyway?" I asked Taylor.

Reaching into his overalls, he took out a silver pocket watch, "Looks to me like a quarta' ta five—can ya stay a spell? We like the company."

"Oh, yeah, I just have a friend with; he's fishing over by the campground. I have a little time then I should get back."

"That's understandable."

Meanwhile, Mabel had cut the fish into smaller pieces and rolled them in flour. "Looks like it's hot enough" – 'ppsshhhhh' went the chunks of fish as she plopped them in the pan of hot oil. As our main course was sizzling away,

Mabel asked, "Do ya like beans? 'Cause we have plenty of 'em. Sometimes we just eat cornbread and beans, but this time, with the fish you caught, we're gonna have us one fine meal."

"Yea, I like beans—sounds good to me."

The meal was ready. There was a stack of blue tin plates—the kind with little white specs all over them. We each grabbed one, helping ourselves to the beans and fried fish.

"Looks like ya done good," Taylor said with his plate full, then sat down on a wooden chair. Off to the side were a couple of car tires lying on the ground. Jacob and I both took one for a place to sit, while Mabel got comfortable in an old rocking chair. "Tastes even better," Taylor said while chewing on a piece of fish and licking his fingers.

"Yeah, it's really good," I told Mabel.

"Why, thank you," she smiled.

Jacob was quiet and content just keeping his mouth full and filling his belly. Taylor, still hungry, got up and put more fish on his plate. "I told ya she could cook good. Yes sa, I'm eatin' more while the eatins' good. Standing next to the camp stove, he finished the meal and put the plate in a bucket of soapy water. "I think I'm gonna do some catfishing tonight," he said, while he filled a corncob pipe with tobacco. "Looks like ittl' be a good night for 'em," as he walked back over to his chair and sat down next to the fire.

"Nuthin' better than smokin' some tobacco afta a good meal." Taylor said, while striking a match and lighting the pipe.

"Yeah it smells good. What kind of tobacco is it?" I asked.

"Oooooh, let's see, well the box says apple, yes sa, apple flava. That's what it is. Da ya want ta try a coupla puffs?"

"Naahh, that's all right, I've got a long trip home and really should get going."

"Jeff, how about I wrap up some of this fish and your friend can have some?" Mabel asked.

"Sounds good, he'll like that."

Taylor pulled his chair a little closer to the fire and started poking around in it with a long stick. "Ya know this here neck of the woods bein' by the riva and all reminds ma of the bayou down south. Yes sa, I don't know wha, somehow it just calls out to ya. Ya get ma meaning?" He pulled the burning stick from the fire and relit his pipe.

"No, I guess I don't."

"Well it's kinda like this down in the bayou along the riva.' It looks all peaceful like and the waters calm but somewhere underneath ya just know there's a big one lurking, waitin' ta get ya."

"You're creeping me out. What do you mean—a big one waiting to get you?"

"Alligata,' yes sa, some times upta fowteen feet long," his eyes gleaming next to the fire.

"Well, there's no alligators up here and what about the woods —is there something in there hiding out?"

Taylor takes a few puffs from the pipe, staring into the fire. "Well," with a pause, "where I come from, we call it 'Swamp Creature' or 'Manbeast.'

Kinda looks like a great big haira' man and stinks awful. Ma saw one years back, yes sa. She was mindin' her own business just washin' dishes afta' suppa'."

"What happened?"

"Well, she was feeling uneasa' at the time, kinda like somethin' was watchin' ova' her."

"Yeah, keep talking."

"Evrathing was dead quiet and still. Pitch black out and notta cricket ta be heard. Kinda like things just got spooked off."

"Then what?" I asked.

"Well I rememba her sayin' the kitchen was hot, so she went ta open the winda in front of the sink. And low and behold, there was the manbeast with its eyes big and starin' in. Yes sa, she plum near died right there. The whole place smelled like skunk, that's ha bad the beast stunk. Then as quiet as it had gotten there so it left. Yes sa, ya just think about that." He emptied tobacco ashes from the pipe and chuckled.

"Ohhh, that's just an old wise tale folks been telling for years. I don't think there's an ounce of truth in it," Mabel said, while wrapping some fish in tinfoil.

"Well, well yes it's been many a year, but folklore is the truth. I believe in the legend and the stora' holds wata', yes sa," Taylor said in a loud voice holding the pipe in one hand and pointing it at her.

"You can believe what you want to," Mabel said handing me the fish.

"Thanks for your hospitality, that was very kind, Jeff."

"Well, thanks for cooking it. Now I don't have to wonder what's for supper."

"You're very welcome."

"Yes sa, Jeff, that was most hospitable and I want ya ta rememba' this where eva' ya go in life, in good times and bad—ya made some true friends here, yes sa."

"Does that mean you have to go, Jeff?" Jacob asked, with sadness in his eyes.

"Yes I do, I've got a long ways to go. Hey, it's okay bud, don't worry, we had fun," I said while untying the daredevil from my fishing line. "Now both of us will have a good memory," as I handed him the lure. "Catch a big one for both of us, okay?"

"Ya sure ya can't stay fer' some catfishing?" Taylor asked.

"Oh no, I need to get home."

"I know, I know, just thought I'd ask is all. Ya take care and we be thinkin' 'bout ya."

Jacob was smiling, looking at the daredevil.

"Yes, Jeff, you have a safe trip home and share some fish with your friend—okay? And our prayers will be with you," Mabel said, while wiping soapy hands on her tattered apron.

"I will. Maybe some day we'll cross paths again. See you later and take it easy," I said, then headed down trail to where the big boulder lay next to the river's edge. When I got there, dusk was setting in and there was a chill in the air. I grabbed my shirt from the tree branch and looked back.

There was Jacob waving with a big smile, "Bye Jeff."

"Goodbye, thank you."

TWENTY-THREE

Mosquitoes and bugs were everywhere in the swampy marsh. I had no bug spray and slid on my shirt to protect me from the biting critters. With my pole in one hand and fried fish in the other, I walked the shoreline once again through the jungle-like growth, which was now dry but thick with insects. When finally out of the woods and onto the campground, I saw Dan upriver, casting away from a dock. In front of me was the go-kart. I walked over, setting my fishing pole and the cooked pike next to it, then sat down. Seeing that I was back, Dan walked over.

"Hey, what's up? Any luck?" I asked.

"Not really, just a few perch and a small bass—nothing worth keeping. How about you? I was wondering where you took off to."

"Oh, I ran into some friends and hung out a while. Caught a good size pike, too."

"Oh yea, where is it?"

"Some of it's right here, you hungry?"

"You know it," Dan answered then sat down.

"Thanks, man, that was good," Dan remarked.

"Yeah, it is. Let's go home."

Dan went behind and pulled the rope, the engine fired, then died. He pulled it again. It fired and ran perfectly. I was in the driver's seat. Dan jumped forwards and sat down, setting the poles in the middle of the seat. "We're outta here!" he shouted. I hit the gas pedal and up the trail we went, passing Walt's and onto the dirt road. It was almost dark by then. Kinda eerie to be way out in the middle of nowhere on a go-kart. The road was bumpy, almost like a washboard. It dipped down deeper into the wilderness, surrounded by tall dark pines that glistened in the moonlight. Ahead of us, we could see the foggy swamp was hovering over the moonlit road. All of a sudden, "Clank, rrrrrrr, as the engine over revved. Oh man, I felt like there was a never-ending pit in my stomach. The engine mount broke and the drive chain fell off. Slowly we came to a stop in the middle of the foggy swamp grass.

"Now what?" Dan asked.

"Looks like it's gonna be a long night. We'll have to take turns pushing while the other one steers."

"That's just great."

Right then, we saw a pair of eyes glowing in the darkness and coming towards us.

"Oh boy!"

"What?" Dan asked.

"I think the swamp creature is coming to get us."

"Man, would you shut up—I don't need to hear that!"

All of a sudden, headlights shined from over the hill and behind the glowing eyes.

"What do you think it is?" Dan asked me.

"I don't know, but if it gets any closer, I'm gonna get the heck out of here!"

About then, the eyes stopped, and so did the headlights. Then, the lights began coming closer. We stood there, scared, in the moonlight, when all of a sudden, the headlights were upon us.

"Hey boys, are you okay?" What are you doing way out here?" To our relief, it was old Walt. "Looks like ya done broke down," he said, while looking out the old pickup truck window. "Do you want a lift home?"

"Man, we sure do. What are you doing out here?" I asked Walt.

"Well, my old hunting buddy Sport got off his chain and took off."

Sport was sitting in the passenger side of the pickup with his tongue hanging out and panting away. "You guys just put that contraption in the back of my truck and I'll give ya a ride home." We did so and got back in the early morning hours.

TWENTY-FOUR ❧

The grass in the backyard was longer than ever. It was warm and sunny out with a slight breeze. Each gust of wind made the once yellow dandelions shed their fluffy tops, like tiny parachutes landing in the field below. The go-kart, along with fishing kept me busy, and I had forgotten to mow the lawn.

I was about halfway done when I saw a small, black pickup truck pull into the driveway. Curious to see who it was, I shut the lawnmower off and walked up the backyard. Both doors opened at the same time and there they were, my grandma and grandpa, all the way from Montana.

"Hi Jeff," Grandma said, while grabbing her purse and pushing the door closed. She put the strap over her shoulder and looked around. "Nice day out. How've ya been?"

"Pretty good."

Grandpa got out and shut the door. He coughed and cleared his throat, "Mowin' the lawn?"

"Yea, I'm almost done."

He pulled out a pack of Lucky Strike cigarettes from his shirt pocket and took out the last one. "Looks like we need to pick up a carton or two, Alma." he said, while lighting it up.

"I have a few left in my purse."

"Naah, I don't like them with the filters."

Mom came out the back door and down the stairs, walked over to Grandma and they gave each other a hug. You could just see the love in Grandma's eyes. I could tell she was happy to see Mom. She had a huge smile and her glasses nearly fell off as they hugged, "Why you, how have you been?"

"Oh good, good and yourself?"

"Oh good, just left yesterday. It was a long drive."

"I bet," then Mom walked over and hugged Grandpa. "Hi Dad! How ya doin'?"

"We're good. How's my pumpkin?"

"Ahh, I'm hanging in there. Why don't we go inside and have some coffee?"

"Sounds good," Grandma answered.

Just then, Irvin pulled up in his old beat up Dodge station wagon and got out. "Alma, well I'll be. And Jim, how are you doin'?"

"Good, what ya' been up to?" Grandpa answered.

"Well, I got a few truckloads of chicken manure I plowed into the garden and I was just on my way back from the farmers' auction. Then I saw everyone here."

Just then, Dad came out the basement door, "Hey, what's goin' on, a family reunion?"

"There he is!" Irvin said loudly.

"How's everyone? Long time—no see," Dad said.

"Good, good—How are you?" Grandpa and Grandma asked.

"I'm good. Same ol', same ol' but different day—ya know."

"Well, why don't I go in and get the coffee pot going," Mom told everybody while walking towards the back porch.

"Fresh coffee sounds good, Janie. Let me come in and give ya' a hand," said Grandma, as they went up the stairs and into the kitchen.

"Go on in and get comfortable and I'll be right up," Dad said as he walked down the side of the house and into the basement.

Everyone pulled out a chair and gathered around the dining room table. "Looks like the coffee's done," Grandma said, as she came over and filled the already placed cups.

"Why, thank you, Alma. Sit down, it's been awhile," said Irvin.

"You're welcome. Yes, it has been awhile," she said, while setting down the coffeepot and taking a seat.

Irvin blew on his cup of steamy coffee to cool it then took a sip, "Good coffee, Jane."

"Thanks. I just remembered I baked some cookies the other day. We'll have them, too."

"Mmmmm, what kind?" Irvin asked.

"Chocolate chip."

"One of my favorites, and if you made 'em I know they'll be good."

"Well, I think they turned out okay. You can be the judge." Mom smiled as she brought the plate of cookies over and sat next to Grandma.

"Well, Jim, what brings you back here?" Irvin asked Grandpa.

"Ohhhh, had to come and see how everyone's doin' and pick up a few things for my logging outfit. Yeah, I'm afraid it's gonna be a short visit. A friend of mine has a couple circular saw blades and an electric motor for the lathe."

"That's good in these times. It's important to have a trade you can fall back on when times get tough," Irvin said, while chewing a cookie and washing it down with several gulps of coffee.

"Yeah, I'll give it a go. Log homes are the thing these days and the saw mills all have their doors closed, so there's no work to be had in that valley."

"Well, I'm sure that things will go good for you," Irvin sipped more coffee.

"We'll make do. Jim's been keeping up with things so it's gonna be fine," Grandma said.

Just then Dad walked in, taking his place at the table. "Yeah, I just cleaned out the woodstove, then I heard everyone pull in. So, what's cookin'?" Dad asked.

"I was just tellin' Irv here about the log lathe."

"Is it going good?"

"Yeah, just came back to say 'Hi,' and get some things done."

"Cool beans," Dad joked.

"Dear, want some coffee?" Mom asked.

"No, I'm okay, thanks though." He turned to Grandma, "So how've ya been, Alma? Have you been keeping busy?"

"Sure, when I'm not weeding the garden I go out back in the Bitterroot River, fly-fishing. Yep, last week I caught a nice sized brown trout—it's in the freezer as we speak—and a couple cutthroat trout Jim and I had for supper that evening."

"Nothing like having that nice river out back, right Alma?" Irvin asked.

"Well, you can catch a meal anytime you want to," she said.

"You sure can. I've eaten more than I can remember," Grandpa said.

"Yep, it must be nice—fresh trout whenever ya want, right Mom?" Mom asked Grandma.

She just smiled and said, "I guess so."

Usually quiet around company, I just sat back and listened while I enjoyed a chocolate chip cookie. It was more crunchy and crumbly, not melting in my mouth like fresh from the oven, but never the less, just as tasty as ever. The story Grandpa told about the log lathe was interesting but when Grandma mentioned the Bitterroot River, it reminded me more of my fishing trip to Walt's and how the motor mounts on the go-kart needed to be welded in place.

Right then from the bedrooms above, I heard a door open and someone coming down the long flight of stairs in a hurry, through the living room and into the kitchen. It was my younger sister Sherry.

"Hi Grandpa and Grandma!" she said happily.

"Well, how's my pumpkin-eater?" Grandpa asked her.

"I'm okay."

"You've grown quite a bit since we last saw you!"

"Yea, she has!" Grandpa remarked as Sherry sat down between them contently. "Where's Blackie?" That was Grandpa's nickname for Kristie because of her black hair. Mom told him that she was taking a nap.

"She's tired and her feet are sore from the corrective shoes the doctor ordered. She should be fine soon. She was walking a little 'pigeon-toed.'"

I felt so bad that my youngest sister had to go through such an ordeal with her feet. It just didn't seem fair. She still smiled though. Maybe she didn't realize what was wrong.

Grandpa reached into his shirt pocket and patted it, "Ahhhh, that's right, I'm out of smokes. Louie, is the Highland Meat Market still around?" he asked Dad.

"Last time I drove by they were. Why?"

"'Cause I need a carton of cigarettes and some other things we can't get out West. Yea, I'm wanting some hard tac and slab bacon and if that bakery is still open, some doughnuts, too."

The Highland Meat Market was a mile or so down the road, a nice little, family-owned, business where you always felt welcome and could get some grub in a pinch, not to mention they had some of the best homemade meats, especially their hotdogs—the tastiest around.

"Well, Alma, let's see what we can find."

"We'll be back in a while. Do you need anything, Janie?" Grandma asked Mom.

"Yea," she said, while fumbling through her purse. "Could you pick up a can of Folgers coffee?"

"Of course we can. Save your money for something else you want."

Sometimes when Mom and I went to the meat market, I would get a smoked whitefish. I loved smoked whitefish and couldn't wait to get home where I would go into the backyard to the big old oak tree. Along side of it was a small maple that I would climb, get comfortable, then eat the fish. Today, my pockets were empty and I knew Dad needed gas money to get to work, so there was no smoked fish to be had. Oh well, maybe next time, I thought.

Irvin yawned and stretched his arms towards the ceiling, "Well, Jeff, come up sometime. I could always use the help. And, Jane, those were good cookies. Louie, you'll have to come up this week. I gotta couple gunny sacks of seed potatoes we have to get in the ground. And, Jane, when the raspberries get ripe, come and get a bunch so you can make some jam."

"I will, thanks," Mom said with a smile.

Since Irvin asked me to stop by, what better timing, I thought to myself. I'm sure he would help fix the go-kart.

TWENTY-FIVE

On the counter top were colorful ice cream cones waiting to be filled. My family and I waited anxiously to try the homemade strawberry ice cream Mom had made the night before. Each of us got to pick what color of cone we wanted. On these occasions, I always chose the green—I just liked the way it looked topped off with two round scoops of ice cream. With our favorite cones in hand, Mom filled them according to our ages, from youngest, being Kristie, to the oldest, which was me. The temperature had climbed into the upper 80s, making every bite of the homemade concoction count. In no time, there were six happy kids at the dining room table, even Kristie with her two top front teeth gone, smacking away at the icy strawberry dessert. Almost done with the ice cream cones, I was saving my favorite part for last. On the cone's bottom was the crunchiest part, savoring each bite of the crunchy cone and ice cream mixture when suddenly I heard Dad shout, "There's a wood chuck in front of the tin shed!"

Downstairs into the basement he ran. Jimmy and I followed. From a cabinet door, Dad grabbed his .22 rifle and took three .22 shells from an old cigar box. His ice cream cone was upstairs waiting to be eaten but this was more important. There had been holes dug all over in the backyard and this was the critter responsible for them. Loaded and ready, Dad fired all three shots...zing!... zing!... zing! The bullets flew close but missed their mark. Startled, the fat varmint scurried under the shed's raised floor.

Both Dan and I had finished our chores at home. Grandma and Grandpa were running around town looking for hard-to-find sawmill parts. Hoping we could convince Irvin to help us, we had just pushed the go-kart a couple of miles and were now in his driveway.

"Is he even home?" asked Dan.

"I'm sure he's around. Hmm... his car is here. I'm sure he's around here somewhere," hoping myself.

I opened the loose fitting, worn out screen door. It slammed behind me. Inside was his sister Louise, with the old cast iron cook stove going.

"What brings you here today?" she asked while opening the oven door and checking loaves of bread inside.

"Oh, I was just wonderin' what Irvin was doing."

The smell of fresh bread and wood smoke filled the kitchen area, making your mouth water even if you were full from supper.

"Oh, I think he's back working with the honeydew. It got pretty warm out there today. Good thing this basement stays cool enough. The cook stove—I'm used to it. We used to use it for everything. I think that it's better than all these new ones they're coming out with, and it warms the house during winter months."

Right then I remembered Irvin and me picking those rutabagas and turnips that cold winter day. How good the kitchen must have smelled with the ham bone boiling.

"Do you really think he's going to help us?" asked Dan, with hope in his voice.

"Yea, I'm very sure. Irvin likes working on stuff like this."

Anxiously, we walked toward the field looking for him. When we reached the white boxes, it looked like Irvin was no where to be found. I hoped myself we didn't push the go-kart all this way not to get Irvin's help. Suddenly towards the end of the row of boxes, I saw a puff of white smoke. There was Irvin all dressed up in a white canvas-like suit with a screen mask covering his face. I wonder what he's up to now. Surprised to see us, he stood up with his smoldering bag.

"What's on your mind today?"

"Oh nothing. We just came by to see how you're doing."

"Good timing. I am checking on how much honey the bees have made so far. To do that, I have to put them to sleep with this canister of smoke."

Reaching the top of the box that sheltered the bees, he pulled out a sheet of beeswax. The honeycomb were partially filled with the sweet nectar.

"Looks like it's going to be a good season if another bear doesn't get into the beehives," he said, while holding up the beeswax. "You boys should save your money and get some bees. It's practical and you could sell the honey."

Irvin talked like that often. With that said, I almost didn't want to ask for help. I was sure we were going to hear about that the whole time.

Irvin pushed the tray back into its slot.

"Okay you boys, what's really on your mind?"

"Well, we were just wondering if you could help us fix something."

"Okay, what is it?" asked Irvin.

"Our go-kart broke down; it needs to be welded."

"What broke on it?"

"We hit a bump and the engine mounts cracked."

"Okay, let me put my things away and I will take a look at it."

What a relief... Irvin was going to help us without a lecture. As we walked towards the driveway I noticed the crop of corn had grown higher and the smell of chicken manure lingered in the air.

Down below was the local Dairy Delight, a place where people sat outside and had ice cream. That summer Irvin's phone rang off the hook about the foul odor of the chicken manure. Irvin wasn't trying to bother anybody and didn't understand why people would complain. The farm had been in his family since the 1800s, and that's how they fertilized the garden.

Looking out into the field, I remembered a story Uncle Stuart told me one time about how a moose ran into the field below, full of arrows. It looked like a pin cushion. The huge animal was butchered right there, not even a block from where the Dairy Delight now sits.

"Corn needs a lot of nitrogen. The manure is the best thing for fertilizer. If the weather holds up, it should grow knee high by July. If I get a good crop this summer, I'll sell some of it and maybe I'll make enough to buy seed for next year."

"Where will you sell it?" I asked.

"I have a stand next to the road with a sign that says 'Corn For Sale.' You should tell your mom to come over soon. The raspberries are almost ripe, and I know she wanted some to make jam. My squash is comin' along good; I'll sell some of those too. They taste best if you bake them in the oven with butter and brown sugar. Okay, let me put my things away and I'll be out in a few minutes."

Irvin walked into the farmhouse. Dan and I waited next to the go-kart. In the front yard grew a huge apple tree with bright red roses growing next to it. The big timbers we'd cut with the two-man saw for firewood were almost gone. All that remained were a few scrap pieces with patches of sawdust in the lawn.

"Hey, look at all those apples." The tree was loaded with green apples about the size of marbles. I always loved the taste of green apples before they were ripe. These were smaller than I liked them, but they were there for the picking. Each of us grabbed a handful and sat next to the well which was behind the rusty old mailbox.

"Man! These are bitter," Dan grimaced with his lips puckered. I chewed mine. They were bitter but I liked them just the same—a touch of salt wouldn't be bad.

"Hey, I wonder if there's water in here," I pumped the well's handle. All that came out was a single cup full of rusty looking water.

"You guys ready? I just had a piece of bread and butter Louise made. It's hot from the oven. Yea, that old well—I haven't used it for a while. Those apples are best when they're ripe."

"What kind are they?"

"They're pie apples. They make the best homemade pie and apple sauce. Well, bring that contraption into the garage," Irvin said, while motioning with his arms. Dan steered while I pushed. In front of the garage door was a big pile of scrap steel; some of it was from cars, old pieces of pipe from plumbing, and other odds and ends.

"Why don't you boys dig through the scrap pile and find what you need." Grabbing a key chain and unlocking the door, "I'll just go in the garage and get things ready." While sliding the big door open, Irvin said, "I'll see if the welder is working. Sometimes, this time of day, everyone is using power so we might be low on electricity." One time we were welding and the lights dimmed. It was during peak hours so we had to stop our project and wait.

Anxiously we dug through the assortment of scrap metal. It was cooler out now as the sun shined partially through the big pines surrounding the old farm house.

"I don't want to be here too long. Let's just find what we need and get it fixed," Dan said while moving an old radiator.

"All right!" I agreed, but somehow in the back of my mind, if I knew Irvin well enough, he wouldn't see a job done half right.

Just then, "Jeff...Jeff," Dan whispered. I looked. A big cotton tail rabbit hopped into plain view, eating long, tender, green, grass and clover next to the barn's edge. Holding an imaginary rifle, "POW! That rabbit would be supper if I had my .22," Dan said.

Right then, on the bottom of the pile lay two pieces of steel; I grabbed them, "These will do the job." Paying no more attention to the rabbit we hurried into the garage.

"Did you find what you need?"

"Yes, these two pieces look like they'll work well."

"It seems we have enough juice for the welder. Looks like both ends should be cleaned up a little so they fit proper," Irvin remarked, while flipping on the big, bench grinder.

It was quite loud. The grinding stone whirled. There was no use trying to talk over it. Dan and I just watched as red sparks lit up the dimmed garage with each grind. I looked above at the clock which had the 'Pabst Blue Ribbon' logo across its front. It was five minutes before six o'clock.

While Irvin ground away, a thought came to my mind about the bear that got into the beehives—"There should be enough time…" (the thought was mine and mine alone). I knew the go-kart engine mounts needed to be fixed so I put the thought aside for now.

"There we go, let's take the motor off and see how it fits."

There were only four bolts holding the 7.5 horse power engine in place, so removing it was easy. Since the old mounts broke underneath, we flipped the go-kart upside down. Next to the welder was a long, workbench with many tools laid out on top of it. Irvin fumbled through them and got two vice grip pliers then quietly walked back over to us.

"There, Jeff, hold these pieces in place." I held the new engine mounts in place while Irvin secured them with the vice grips.

"It looks like they fit pretty good, Jeff. Good thing we cleaned up the ends." Having put on the welding mask, bright ultraviolet lights and the unmistakable smell of welding, and the bright sparks, reminded me of sparklers on the Fourth of July.

"We'll just let that cool off a bit," Irvin remarked, while putting the welding equipment away.

"We'll be riding the go-kart in no time!"

"Pretty soon," I assured Dan.

"Cool! It looks like it's turning out pretty good."

As the new welds cooled, I walked over to the huge window. The rabbit was still munching away. On the window's ledge lay a pipe for smoking tobacco. It looked like the kind Sherlock Holmes used, covered with a heavy coating of dust and cobwebs. It must have been sitting there for years, I thought.

"I think it's cooled off enough. I'll just chip off the flux."

I was just about to ask Irvin if he wanted the old pipe anymore. On second hand, he had already helped us with the go-kart. I am sure he would have parted with the old pipe, but I didn't want to ask for to much.

The anticipation of driving the go-kart grew as we watched Irvin scrub the remaining flux with a wire brush.

"Well, your contraption's fixed. I still don't know what you see in this thing," I could go on and tell Irvin how much fun it was to ride, but that was just Irvin saying and doing things in his own time; kind of like 'slow and steady wins the race.' He was just making sure things were done as good as could be or as he saw fit.

On some days I'd skip school and hang out on the farm with him. After almost a full day, he would finally ask, "Don't you belong in school today?" My reply was always, "I'm on lunch break," but I'm sure he knew better and never questioned it. He would just ask that I call headquarters so my parents knew where I was. I guess that's why I loved dropping by so much.

With a few turns of the wrench, we finally had the motor bolted in place. "That should hold for a long time. It's extra strong. You can hit all the bumps you want and the engine won't break that mount," Irvin remarked.

With the job done, Dan and I pushed the go-kart towards the

big garage door. The rear sprocket was in line with the clutch and the chain spun freely. It might have taken a little extra time, but it was going to work great. Just outside, the big door slid closed behind us and the ring of keys jingled as Irvin put the weathered pad lock in place. As I watched him lock up, I knew I'd be back soon in the fall. I already knew I'd be glad to stop by and help him harvest the squash, which were now in full bloom with their big orange flower tops. The thought I had was strongly on my mind.

"I should get home soon. Mom's deep frying some chicken for supper," said Dan with hunger in his voice.

"Man, you guys eat so late. Here, I wanna show you something."

"Will it take long? I'm starving!"

"No."

"What is it?"

"You'll see."

Dan let out a big sigh, "I hope it's good."

Silence was in the air except for the sound of the crickets and insects that surrounded the farm. Almost there, we picked up the pace, heading towards the tall willow trees. Spring's rebirth had covered the area with green.

"Hmm… there it is."

"What?"

"That's where we buried the bear Irvin shot." The site was barely noticeable.

"Aah! Let's get going!" Dan didn't seem too excited. But the excitement of Irvin's phone call and the bear was still vivid in my mind.

Would my 20-gauge loaded with slugs be enough power to slay such a beast? The rest of the evening was spent in my room reading *Field and Stream*, *Outdoor Life*, and *Cartridges of the World* and dreaming of hunts soon to come.

TWENTY-SIX

The wet gravel crunched under my hiking boots. Little muddy pools of water filled the washed out spots on the dirt road I'd take as a short cut back and forth to work. I'd landed a job at a local high school doing custodial work and was now on my way home. It had just rained, steam rose from the blacktop street ahead. It was a hot muggy day; the downpour left a fresh smell and cooled the neighborhood. After putting in a good day, walking home was too tiring and cumbersome.

I'd reached the short cut's end and was now on the main drag. It looked like a motorcycle was for sale in a driveway. I stopped to have a look. Hmm… a Yamaha 250 Enduro, fully equipped with speedometer, headlight and turn signals. This would be easy on gas and fun. It would sure beat walking to work. I'd just sold my beater Chevy pick-up and soon due for my next pay check. I think I can swing it; I still had the urge to ride. Here we go—'wheelin and dealin' again.

Well, here I was in the driveway, cleaning the spark plugs and air cleaner and adjusting the points on my new form of transportation. I worked out a good deal and had a few bucks to spare for gas and oil. I was back home after spending some time in the small town of Darby, Montana, with my Aunt Kate, Aunt Vicky, Uncle Jerry and four cousins: Jimmy, Jeri Lynn, Dawn, and Trish. It is a small town nestled between a snow-capped mountain and a grassy foothill with a big letter "D" made from rocks that were white washed. Even on the hottest days the Bitterroot

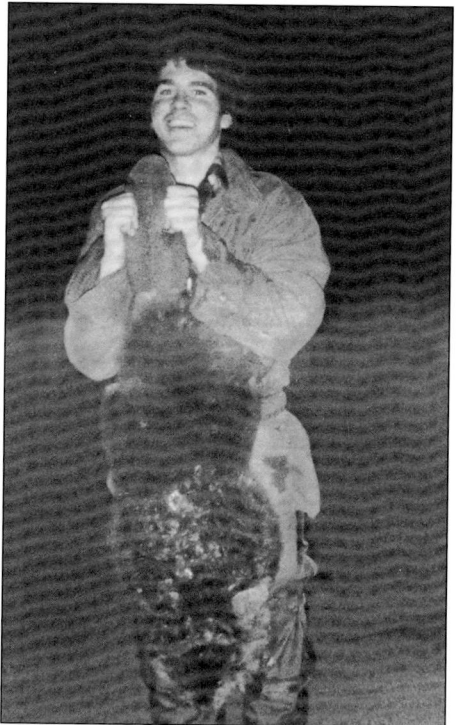

Jeff with a beaver he trapped in Montana.

115

River ran icy cold through the small town, known as the Bitterroot Valley.

My stay there was most memorable. Cousin Jimmy, Uncle Jerry, and I trapped beaver, bob cat, and pine martin on the mountain above, known as Trapper's Peak. Uncle Randy, Kate's husband, hurt his back while helping Uncle Jerry fill the big logging truck. He was no longer able to work, so there I was, a lumberjack at seventeen.

Grandpa's lathe turned out some of the best timber in its day. We worked all summer to keep up the demand for log homes. The work was sixteen to seventeen hour days—hard, honest, and tiring. At breakfast we had elk steak, fried brook trout that Jimmy and I caught in Tincup Creek, pancakes, and we would fry potatoes that Uncle Jerry grew in his garden he was so proud of. Often times, after a hard day's work, I plopped into bed, completely exhausted. Morning came too soon and I would awake in the same position; it felt great! I was doing a man's job at my young age of seventeen and bought my first car.

I'd finished eleventh grade at Darby High School. My custodial work was not even comparable or as fulfilling as my logging job out West, I thought to myself, while polishing car wax from the motorcycle's tank.

This summer was a blast. Dennis, Jimmy, and I practically lived on our motorcycles. All we cared about was having enough money to fill the gas tanks. One day that summer we cut through Irvin's field. My brother Jimmy and I were ahead of Dennis. We just parked close by a smelly, giant pile of chicken manure, waiting to be spread out. The sound of Dennis' new Kawasaki 250 was growing closer. In a moment, Dennis appeared. Running through the gears, he barreled downhill. Both Jimmy and I wondered what he was doing. Not even a half a minute later Dennis was up to his handle bars in foul smelling chicken manure. Wrestling the bike from the pile of foul smelling stench, we heard every cuss word imaginable, as I'm sure the neighbors did too.

"Why didn't you guys tell me it was chicken manure? I thought it was a dirt pile!" He shouted while knee deep.

Steam rolled off the exhaust pipe and cooling fins on the dirt bike's engine. The foul stench of the wet chicken manure was enough to make you gag. It was pretty funny how Dennis had mistaken the pile of chicken manure for dirt. He was pretty hot under the collar and with the look on his face, we tried not to laugh. It was then that all of us agreed to take a spin up to Air Base Pond. Jimmy on his Kawasaki 125, which Dad helped him find a good deal on, and I took off first. We wanted to be well ahead of Dennis and for a good reason. It was quite hot out, and the wind felt great as we shifted through the gears down and old back road. Almost at the road's end I was nailed in the forehead by a big, fat grasshopper. I slowed down and pulled over, the grass hopper was wedged inside my helmet.

With the huge smashed bug out of my helmet, I picked up the pace again. Just ahead, the whole width of the road had been bulldozed out about five feet deep. It was to prevent traffic from going through, but that didn't stop us. We just made a new trail right through it. A street not traveled much crossed ahead about a hundred feet. It was uphill, I could see there were no cars going by. First, second, third… I sped up. It was like a jump, I cleared most of the pavement, landing on the other side. The trail sloped down and was swampy. I down-shifted into second, gave it some gas, and rode a wheelie through a fifty foot puddle of water. Jimmy and Dennis were fast behind. It was fun racing by the ditch along the roadside.

The trail leveled off for a ways then sloped back down. Cool! A nice muddy spot! I'm just gonna slow down until they catch up. I crossed, going even slower. Then, with both of them close, I cracked the throttle. The rear tire spun through the black muck. I was just having fun, hoping to give them a good coating of the sticky, black goop. We pulled this on each other all the time, trying to make it look like an accident.

"Man, what did you do that for?" they both shouted.

"I need enough power to get through!" I shouted, while laughing on the inside.

We passed each other off and on, doing whatever to stay in the lead. About fifteen minutes later we ended up passing two open gates reading, Rice Lake Landfill. Side-by-side we slowed down, being cautious. Looked like the coast was clear, there were no dump trucks in the area.

The gravel road was slightly damp. Going fast was no problem as we raced onward. Up on our right was a small toll booth. With a quick glance, I looked in the window. Usually there was someone inside to collect a fee, depending on how much and what kind of junk you brought. We passed the second set of gates that led into the heart of the dump. Hundreds of seagulls and crows flocked everywhere, making their bird-like sounds, while picking at the ripe, but smelly ground. The odor lay heavy in the air. On our left were old refrigerators, laundry machines, and kitchen ovens. We flew past. It was hot out that day. The road stretched upwards for quite a ways. Tuning the engine on my 250 had paid off. The power was strong and crisp. I went through every gear without even the slightest sputter. No sooner had I reached the top, I looked up the road. It sloped down gradually, which looked like about a half a mile.

"Cool! Let's see how fast I can get going!"

The speedometer read sixty-five. I could feel the wind's resistance under my helmet and visor. My eyes watered from the strong wind. My motorcycle boot found the shifter on the left and tapped it into fifth gear. There should be enough length of the road, I thought to myself. I was at seventy-five mph. The speedometer's needle kept climbing… seventy-eight, then seventy-nine. In the excitement, at almost eighty, the road ran short. Dust flew and gravel kicked up from the tires. I used the front and rear brakes softly and down shifted, but it was no use, I had missed the corner. I plundered through the field, my teeth grit, hoping not to hit any obstacles hidden in the tall grass. At that time, I thought my bike would be not more than a launch pad and I would be sailing through the air. I finally brought the bike to a stop. Thank God I didn't run into anything. I looked back and here comes Jimmy and Dennis. They followed the same, almost disastrous route that had taken me off course.

"Man, what are you guys doing? The only reason I'm out here is because I was going too fast and missed the corner." I had to laugh at them even though I was shaken up from the rough ride.

Suddenly my brother Jimmy started laughing uncontrollably and said, "Look at Dennis!" Dennis had wet toilet paper stuck on his jean jacket and helmet and was spitting something from his mouth. On their way down, Jimmy swerved and hit a puddle in the sewage dumping area. The motorcylce had plunged through and it's tires splashed the foul water high into the air with Dennis right behind him, catching toilet paper and all.

"That does it! I've had enough! Let's go!" Dennis said, exasperated, while wiping his face with his shirt sleeve.

Our original plan was to take a swim in the pond nearby. We left and in no time at all we reached the front gates. Upon arriving there was a surprise that lay ahead. The Rice Lake County Sheriff was waiting for us.

"Okay boys, you know better than to ride on the streets. You better have a good excuse."

Trying to sound convincing, "We've always riden our bikes on this road." Playing dumb didn't seem to help us at all.

"Come here you guys. Looks like I'm going to have to impound your bikes and call a wrecker." He took down our names.

"Aww, can't you just give us a break?"

He sat smug in his patrol car with a smirk on his face. "I don't think so, and as soon as your buddy gets down here, I'll get his name too." It seemed like nothing was going to change his mind.

Dennis crossed the street and pulled up, "What's going on?"

Jimmy and I told him that the sheriff had written our names down and he was going to call the wrecker, and he wanted Dennis' name too.

Suddenly, there was a gust of wind. The foul stench of chicken manure and sewage filled the air.

"Okay boys, on second thought, I got things to do. I'm just going to let you off with a warning. Stay off the streets now," the sheriff warned us as he backed out and went down the road.

Jimmy and I broke out in laughter.

"What are you guys laughing at?"

"Ahhhhh! The sheriff took off because of the smell!"

Dennis was dumb-founded. Little did he know that he had saved the day!

Well, the three of us spend a good hour at the pond, just goofing around, care free. We road our motorcycles through the shallows, letting the spring fed water splash clean the muck off of our tires. It was hot out. After putting the kickstand down, I kicked off my boots, took off my jean jacket and flannel and threw them into a pile with my wallet. Stepping into the cool water, I waded about waist deep and dove under, blue jeans and all. It felt great! Cleansing off a few hours of dust and sweat. Jimmy put on a pair of swim trunks. Dennis dove in, in hopes of getting the dry crust off his jeans. It was summer; we had all the time in the world. It seemed no sooner than we were there, we hit the trail again. Almost half way home, Jimmy's bike sputtered and came to a stop. Dennis and I waited as he kicked it over with no luck.

"What's the problem?" Jimmy mumbled to himself. After unsnapping the seat and lifting it; there was the cause. The engine's cleaner had sucked in his swim trunks, choking the carburetor off.

The three of us had just crossed the rocky boundary by the Dairy Delight and crossed Arrowhead Road. The big yellow gate on the bottom of Irvin's garden was open, next to the corn stand he had built. We blasted pass. There sat Irvin on his tractor with his railroad cap on, puttering across his field. The pile of chicken manure was now flat and worked into the garden soil. He didn't wave, maybe he just didn't see us, or was lost in his own world, doing what he enjoyed so much.

Down the dirt road and through the hilly backwoods, we rode. We just passed our Great Uncle Ed's field with the small apple tree in it. The sun shone bright with an orangeish sky above. Soon we would be going up the backyard on the trail alongside the garden.

L.C., Taylor, Mable, and Jacob, and the story of the man-beast—well, doesn't every boy have an imagination? Dennis, Jimmy, and I just passed the old oak tree and Dad was tilling the garden. You know all the stories that Irvin told me that happened in his day of seventy plus years. That old oak tree must have been two or three hundred years old. Just think if it could speak—what a tale it could tell!

Dad tilling the garden near the old oak tree.

Sometimes in life when things get too tough or hectic, I think back to the simple joys of my childhood. Time goes much too fast. I remember when I was ten years old, I told my mom that I just wanted to be older and do all the 'grown-up' things. At the time, she was folding clothes and said, "When you grow up, you sometimes wish you could be a kid again".

Take a moment and think about it—remember your first shack, digging worms to go fishing, or hunting for the first time; how new and exciting it was. One time my Great Uncle Art sat at the kitchen table and told my parents that when he was a kid, if somebody told him, "You're going to live to be eighty years old," he wouldn't have believed it. "I'm eighty-three now. It doesn't seem so long ago," he commented over coffee.

How true it is. I see it myself now that I'm older. Precious are the memories of my youth and our home. It was a time when my family was together and a place where I could run free in the backyard. Our home—a safe place—a haven that sheltered us.

Irvin is gone now but his memory lives on. A good friend found him on the living room floor with his Rosary clenched in his hands. His time had passed.

The last time I saw him I was at home in my van. He looked into the side window, half shouting, "Jeff, when are you gonna get out of that wheelchair and help me in the garage!" I'm sure he didn't realize the extent of my injury. I wanted to answer back so desperately but was on a ventilator at the time which left me with no voice. He was hard of hearing and surely couldn't hear my faint whisper.

My brother, four sisters, and I got to know him so well. We grew up knowing him as Uncle Irvin; a kind friendly man always willing to help anyone, whether it be fixing something, plowing driveways with his tractor, teaching what he knew or sharing vegetables from his garden. It's been many years since the car accident that left me paralyzed: I still remember it all.

Precious are the memories of my youth. Why? When my condition gets overwhelming, I can reflect on those days to make the day go by.

Often times a young person will ask, with a twinkle of curiosity in their eyes, "Jeff, how did it used to be?" or "Could you help me fix this?" In an instant I see myself at that age, asking the same kinds of questions to my old friend, Uncle Irvin.

Jeff's friend "Uncle" Irvin.

Jeff with a new pair of snowshoes.

Jeff taking his little sister Kristie for a ride.

Jeff happy to get a new bow and arrow set for his birthday. Pictured with his brother Jimmy and his cousin Jimmy.

Jeff and Jimmy with their new BB guns.
L to R: Annette, Jackie, Sherry, Jimmy, Jeff.

Jeff loved to fish.

Jeff with his siblings on Christmas morning. L to R, top to bottom:
Jackie, Jeff   Annette, Jimmy   Sherry, Kristie

Jeff not long before the accident.

Jeff's high school graduation photograph, 1982.

Grandmaison photo